TITUS BRANDSMA
A Modern Martyr

Joseph Rees

SIDGWICK & JACKSON
LONDON

First published 1971
Copyright © 1971 Sidgwick & Jackson Limited

I.S.B.N. 0.283.97817.1

Printed in Great Britain
by Morrison & Gibb Ltd, Edinburgh
for Sidgwick and Jackson Limited
1 Tavistock Chambers, Bloomsbury Way
London W.C.1

Contents

Illustrations

Acknowledgements

The present book is based, almost exclusively, on the Dutch standard work by H. W. F. Aukes.

Until recently Mr H. W. F. Aukes was a Director of the Catholic Residential College for Catholic Adult Education at Witmarsum in the Netherlands. He is also Chairman of the European Committee for Catholic Adult Education and Ecumenism, and a member of the Praesidium of the FEECA – the overall organization for Catholic Adult Education in Europe.

He was a personal friend of Titus Brandsma, as well as a distant relative, and, as a scientific assistant at the library of the Catholic University of Nijmegen, he worked with him for the last three years of his life.

Aukes first published his biography in 1947, but was careful to explain that it was not a comprehensive work for he had been forced to collect the material for it during the war years. After the war, more evidence became available and the present Postulator and Vice-Postulator in the cause of Titus Brandsma's beatification were able to supply him with additional material.

So, in 1961, Aukes was able to publish what the Postulator could, with confidence, claim to be a definitive biography: *Het leven van Titus Brandsma*, published by Het Spectrum, Utrecht/Antwerpen.

Joseph Rees, who has produced this shortened English version, is himself working as a priest in England. While in Holland he obtained an interview with H. W. F. Aukes and the Vice-Postulator and was given their fullest co-operation.

He also undertook a journey to Dachau to acquaint himself more fully with Brandsma's final destination.

He would like to thank Malachy Lynch, O.Carm., for recalling his personal memories of Titus Brandsma so clearly and helpfully, and for allowing them to be included here. He would also like to thank the Carmelite nuns at Ware for their accounts of, and illuminating comments on, the historical background of the Carmelite Order.

He owes a special debt of gratitude to Margaret Pantling of St Margarets, Herts., for generously offering her services as a typist.

He would also like to thank Clonmore and Reynolds Limited for permission to quote from *The Beauty of Carmel* by Titus Brandsma as well as for permission to quote one or two references from *A Dangerous Little Friar* by Josse Alzin.

Preface

The man about whom this book is written was a Dutch Carmelite priest. He was also a journalist who wrote hundreds of articles and was, for a short time, the editor of a local newspaper. He held a degree in philosophy, became professor at the University of Nijmegen, and was elected the Rector Magnificus of that University for the academic year of 1932.

He was also a mystic, though rather a scientific one. It was said of him, with some truth, that he was the only mystic in the continent of Europe who held a railway season ticket. As someone jokingly remarked, he became a saint from spending so long in trains.

In his book, *Co-responsibility in the Church*, Cardinal Suenens wrote that Christ was so completely given to men only because He was so completely given to God. This truth is, at last, beginning to register on the Christian mind. But although the appeal for involvement finds an increasingly ready response, the religious spirit that man should bring to it is often lacking, or strangely feeble and precarious.

But in Titus Brandsma we have, perhaps, a prototype of what we could be. For his eyes reflected his soul and his fellow men rediscovered in this 'child of man' the rare beauty of what it means to be also a 'child of God'. Even some of his guards in prison and the concentration camp were not immune to its effect.

The following pages will try to show a man who was much in love with life, who appreciated all the good things it offered, who was enthralled by its potentialities and preoccupied with its needs.

They will also show us that he was a man who understood the special problems and aspirations of our time and so won the confidence and affection of the young.

In life, Titus Brandsma's nature and grace were so closely integrated that it was difficult to draw the line between them; just as in death the facts suggest that he gave his life both for God and for his country.

The message and relevance of his life are that they invite us, if not to follow suit, to feel the same attraction and to undergo the same fusion of nature and grace.

JOSEPH REES

Important dates in the life of Titus Brandsma

23 February 1881	Anno Sjoerd Brandsma born at Oegeklooster, (Frisia), Holland.
4 May 1892	First Holy Communion.
September 1892	Boarding school at Megen.
September 1898	Entered the Carmelite Noviciate at Boxmeer.
17 June 1905	Ordained Priest.
1906–9	Rome.
1909–23	Oss (teaching philosophy).
1923–42	Nijmegen.
1932–33	Rector Magnificus of the Catholic University at Nijmegen.
19 January 1942	Arrested.
19/20 January 1942	In the prison at Arnhem.
20 January–12 March 1942	In the prison at Scheveningen.
12 March–28 April 1942	In the concentration camp at Amersfoort.
16 May–13 June 1942	In the transitory prison at Kleve (Germany).
19 June–26 July 1942	In the concentration camp at Dachau (Germany).

PART ONE

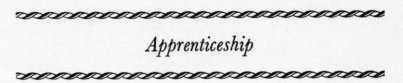

Apprenticeship

Chapter One

CHILDHOOD AND YOUTH

The story of Titus Brandsma's life begins in Frisia (Friesland), a province in the very north of Holland. Here, when the nights are not overcast, one can see the lights from the lighthouses on the off-shore islands pointing towards the sky. Like the Welsh, the Frisians have their own language and characteristics. They are known for their reserve, for a certain sternness and reticence which distinguishes them from their fellow countrymen. Yet Anno (who took the name of Titus when he entered the Carmelite Order) was essentially cheerful and optimistic, almost jovial in his response to people and certainly dynamic in his response to life.

But, perhaps, there was an underlying caution, as well as a fierce tenacity of purpose, which owed itself to his long peasant history. For Frisia is by and large an agricultural province; its landscape is flat, its soil fertile clay. The farms are often quite big and its dairy products are no strangers to the British market.

It was on one of these larger farms that, on the 23rd February, 1881, Anno Sjoerd Brandsma was born. His great-grandfather had bought the place at Oegeklooster sixty years before for his eldest son, Henry, Titus's grandfather. His grandmother, Henry's wife, belonged to one of the oldest Frisian families which in recent times have given the Catholic Church some prominent sons.[1]

As far back as one can trace on both sides, Anno's ancestors were farmers: solid, dependable and realistic. He was not unlike them. And his truly Frisian nature is shown further by his toughness in severe weather conditions, his dry comments, and that strong, practical common sense with which he faced the social situations that confronted him.

Shortly before his arrest in 1942, in the middle of a particularly bitter winter, he went out without scarf and coat and, when someone showed concern, laughed it off, saying: 'I am a Frisian, I can take it.'

Anno was deeply attached to the province of his birth.[2] He loved his contacts with the Frisian countryside and was never to lose the simplicity which is characteristic of its people. In his writings he frequently illustrated a point with an apt reference to a farmer's life, and those who once accompanied him on a study-excursion into Frisia won't forget how, standing on a cart in the courtyard of what once had been a Benedictine Abbey, he improvised, for their entertainment as well as their instruction, a re-enactment of work and prayer in those early days.

Anno's mother, Tjitse Postma, was a simple, deeply religious woman. She was not strong though photographs show her to be good-looking and upright; her face was thinned by ill-health and the determination that overcame it; her body was slight and again, in its rigidity, full of resolution. Beauty is not a word to be used lightly, but in some of her photographs she is not without it. Within the family circle she was talkative, though in her care for the children she tended to be anxious and over-meticulous. Like her husband, Anno's father, she gave outsiders the impression of being reserved and rather cold.

Titus, her husband, was a reserved man with a grave, conservative manner, but he was a man one could count on. He was also intelligent, with an interest in things that stretched beyond the farm. He became a member of a local council and chairman of the local Election Board which brought him into regular touch with some well-known Frisians. At home he played the piano and enjoyed teaching his children the songs and local dances of the times. On the whole, theirs was a sober life, and all kinds of reminiscences show that their spirit of prayer went much further than one would expect to find in a solid Catholic home in the countryside of that time.

The Brandsmas' regular journeys to town or country, always made in a horse-drawn cart, were often spent in praying together. During Lent, his mother refused to wear the ornaments that normally adorned the Frisian head-dress, a custom which was by then already dying out. In later days, when they moved to the nearby town of Bolsward, they were to be seen every morning at Mass in the parish church.

In those days it was unusual to go to Communion frequently, but the Brandsmas received Communion several times during the week. They took a firm line of kneeling side by side in church, contrary to the custom of the time. For this was a period when the sexes in church were strictly separated – the men on one side, the women on the other. All this suggests that although they were devout they were not dependent upon current moods and fashions. They held a thinking, forward-looking attitude which was certainly original and must, sometimes, have needed courage.

The Reformation had made the Frisian Catholics more isolated than before, the more so because all communications had to be negotiated across lakes, rivers and ponds. In this environment it is perhaps not altogether surprising to find them more self-confident and resilient in their belief, more free in thought and action, and less addicted to the temptation of an over-organized society. Possibly this played a part in accounting for the fact that so many priests and missionaries came from Frisia. Already in 1880 this province alone counted ten Catholic Boards of Election in contrast to twenty in the remainder of Holland. They were also among the first to found agricultural banks and dairy centres. They certainly lost no opportunity in making the most of the liberty they enjoyed. And the Brandsmas did not lag behind. If they were whole-hearted Catholics, they were also extremely active ones.

Of Titus's grandfather, Henry Brandsma, one fact is noteworthy. In a sad affair concerning ecclesiastical possessions he stepped in determined to resolve the issue. By-passing a parish priest, who held a rather narrow view, he wrote, with a Brandsma's typical frankness, to the Archbishop of Utrecht. He did so at a particularly delicate moment when already some of those involved in similar cases had been barred from the sacraments. But his letter was clearly thought out and succinct. In it he proposed a plan which was to lead to a happy solution.[3]

It is interesting to learn this about the grandfather of a man who
was so often to involve himself in delicate issues and who always
endeavoured to reconcile conflicting views. 'I have the privilege,'
he was later to say, 'to come from a family in which one lived
warmly with everything that advanced the cause of Frisian
Catholics.' 4

Anno's father, like his grandfather, was certainly one of those
who looked ahead and was well aware of the widening fields
of opportunity in Press, education and politics. Without being
prepared for it, almost certainly unable to account for it, he
sensed that perhaps they could be used to render Christ
present to the world.

The Brandsma family was to consist of four girls and two
boys, nearly all of them destined for the religious life. The
eldest daughter, Boukje, joined the Poor Clares. She died in
1939, not long after the death of her younger sister, Siebrig,
who had already been Superior of a convent of the Sisters of the
Precious Blood. Another daughter, Plone, joined the Franciscan
Sisters. Only Gatske eventually married and became Mrs de
Boer. The two boys came last in the family. They were to follow
in the footsteps of their sisters. Anno's younger brother, Henry,
became a Franciscan priest. Their cousin, Gorgonius, who
helped out on the Brandsma farm as a boy, joined the Mill Hill
Society and became Bishop of Kisoemoe in Africa. Later on,
another relative became Bishop of Loeanfoe in China.5 Their
vocations were as far flung as they were united in purpose.

It is not difficult to see why, in this tightly enclosed and
strong-minded society, this should happen. The Brandsma
children had little contact with the outside world. The people
they saw were cousins with whom they must have endlessly
discussed their ideas and ambitions. Mrs Brandsma's inclina-
tions, as well as her ill-health, predisposed her to stay at home.
It did more. It led her to discourage visits from other children,
from anyone outside the home, in fact. This is probably why, in
later years as well, Anno's friends would rarely find their way to
his farm. Not that their life as children was dull. It was too busy
for that in the days when butter and cheese were still made on
the farm itself and when the hours were often long and heavy.

The economic conditions in the eighties weighed heavily on the country and not a few families crashed or managed to keep going only by taking out mortgages, although the Brandsmas were not among them. The children, if they worked on the farm, did so only as casual helpers.

Such was the background to Anno's early years. In the farm-house, which looked out on the church towers of Bolsward and Hichtum, the ancient mantelpiece in one of the rooms depicted Oegeklooster as it had been in the 16th century. Perhaps Anno's conciliatory nature owed more to his past than he himself realized.

He certainly never forgot how one evening his father heard someone moving stealthily round the house and suspected that the intruder was after his apples. Rushing out-side he discovered that the suspect had safely fled under cover of dark. Angrily he returned to the house muttering: 'If I set my hands on him . . . I'll——'

'Just as well you didn't,' interrupted his observant son, 'or know who it was either, come to that.'

The remark amazed and calmed his father. But the incident, small as it was, was probably one of many that account for Anno's constant efforts in the years that followed to take the sting out of explosive situations.

At the time, of course, he was still at school – a small, slightly built boy, but a lively and gay one with a curiously precise intelligence that enabled him to learn with ease and provided him with a good memory as well as an inquisitive mind. His father often read aloud at night to the family, sometimes from history, sometimes from biographies of the great men of the Church, but occasionally, in spite of himself, his thoughts would be occupied with problems left over from the day. When this happened and he failed to remember where he left off on the previous occasion, Anno would call out from behind the doors of his cupboard bed (which was still a usual feature in farm-houses of those days) and refer his father to the last episode of the story.

At home the family spoke Frisian, which is not a dialect but a language. As a man, Anno was to plead to the Ministry in The Hague for its official recognition. Fifty years later he

recalled how astonished he had been when, accompanying his
mother on a visit to the Dean, he heard them conversing together in Frisian, which was not normally associated with the
educated classes and the public life. His years at the primary
school passed without ado except for one small incident. One
day, together with some other children, he was taking French
lessons after school. It was the custom then that each one in
turn would treat the group to a sweet. When Anno's turn came
he refused to do so. It is possible, of course, that times were
difficult and that he wanted to spare his parents this extra
expense. But it is just as likely that it was plain stubbornness, a
Frisian characteristic. Whatever the cause, he would not give
in and they grabbed him and held him under the pump.[6]

It was about this time, his last year at the primary school,
that Anno told his parents of his wish to become a priest. Not
long afterwards his brother, who was only a year younger, was
to come forward with the same idea. To his parents it meant
that neither son would be there to help on the farm and that,
in addition, they would need to provide for at least another
six years for their studies at a boarding school. But they took it
with good grace. It must, after all, have been in accord with
their wishes.

A few months before Anno was to leave home, he made his
first Holy Communion. It was on the 4th May, 1892. He was
eleven years old, the usual age at the time.

During the ceremony, and on behalf of everyone there, Anno
recited the long and difficult Tridentine Profession of Faith. In
fact he knew it by heart and did not have to refer to the formula
once, which was quite an extraordinary achievement. Did he
understand the contents of this Creed which we today would no
longer dream of using? In asking the question one is reminded
of another incident in which the testimonies of his brother and
sister are very positive. In gratitude for a recovery in the family,
Anno and his brother decided to say for a month the Office
of the Virgin Mary. Anno, it is said, strove constantly to understand its meaning.

In September that year Anno left home. He had never
before been outside Frisia. His mother found it hard to see him

go as, from the farm, she watched the steam tram disappearing into the distance. For Anno had already walked to the nearby town of Bolsward where he joined a team of at least another ten boys, among whom were a future navy chaplain and a future musician as well as his cousin, the future bishop in Africa.

Together, they made the journey by tram and train to Megen, a town in the southern and almost exclusively Catholic province of Brabant. There, nearly two and a half centuries ago, the Franciscans had established themselves on the river Maas. Megen is a small town with an old prison tower, a few churches and monasteries and the castle – now occupied by the Poor Clares – and surrounded on all sides by canals. Very old lime trees form a picturesque avenue to the long street used by the Franciscans and their students, and beyond which lies a dyke. The new schoolbuilding, called 'The Latin School', had been in use for six years when Anno arrived.

The hundred and fifteen students were divided between a few selected boarding-houses to which the Franciscans always had free access, a group of about eight to ten students to each with a senior student in charge. Discipline was strict and a rigorous timetable adhered to. The school was intended to serve the purpose of a junior seminary, with the understanding that the boys were still free to choose which particular form of religious life they eventually wished to join. One of the Fathers is said to have remarked to Anno, 'You are too clever to become a Franciscan, you'd better be a Jesuit.' (The Franciscans at that time were mainly preoccupied with pastoral care and a few schools, which was in fact also the case with the Carmelites.)

That Anno did well in his studies comes as no surprise.[7] His special interest lay in history and literature, though, oddly enough, these were not his best subjects. His fellow students recall that he was already 'somebody', a person of character, one who had 'a mind of his own'. He was a good mixer and well liked by his class, which had the reputation of being a difficult one. Perhaps his ducking beneath the pump had taught him more than he realized.

There was nothing specifically wrong with Anno's health, but the prefect noticed that he could do with some extra sleep

and milk. He had clearly inherited his mother's frailty. Once
his father nearly took him back home – this was during his third
year at Megen – but the prefect reassured his father, promising
to keep an eye on Anno and assuring him that the holidays on
the farm would buck his son up. During all this time, Anno
wrote home regularly but, unfortunately, all his letters have
been lost.[8]

During Anno's years at Megen, his eldest sister, Boukje,
joined him there with the Poor Clares at the convent in the
castle. It hardly requires much imagination to see where the
influence came from. The contemplative life must have been
endlessly discussed in the Brandsma home.

During his final years at Megen, Anno began to orientate
himself in regard to the various Religious Orders and the
possibilities that lay before him. He discussed his impressions
with some of his fellow students. But it was not until many
years later, that he described (at a Chapter meeting of the
Dutch Carmelite Province) what had determined his choice.[9]
He had enjoyed his prefect's joke about the Jesuits but had not
taken it seriously, but now, it seemed, his health was to fall in
on the prefect's side – or anyway against the Franciscan calling.
He simply wasn't strong enough to carry out the busy pastoral
life of the Franciscan. He must look elsewhere.

He looked, as we now know, toward the Carmelites. The
very spirituality of the Carmel Order, especially the characteristics of its life of prayer and its special relation to the Mother
of God, drew him strongly.

His parents, however, weren't too pleased with his decision.
At home he had been to the Franciscans for catechism; he had
made his studies at their school. His parents, therefore, had
automatically assumed that he would join them. His mother
even brought pressure on him to change his mind. But Anno
stood his ground. There can be no doubt whatever that the
contemplative aspect of the Carmel Order, combined with its
flexible approach towards apostolic activities, was very attractive
to him.

The Dutch Carmel Province was actively engaged in parish
work and was to concern itself with education as well as with

a mission in Brazil. Anno remarked to his brother that he was pleased that the Carmelites did not work 'in stages'.[10] What exactly he meant by this, we do not know, but we do know that it was the special relation between Carmel and the Mother of God that struck him so forcibly.

He would certainly have read the traditional account of St Simon's vision of Mary in which she casts her cloak about him.* (Whether this occurred at Cambridge or Aylesford is a matter still in dispute with scholars.) He would realize, too, that this was a reminder of an earlier vision in which Elijah was told by God (seven hundred years before the birth of Christ) to go forth and anoint a King and appoint his successor. When he did so, however, Elijah found his successor ploughing a field with twelve yoke of oxen. So he went up behind him in his furrow and flung his garment over him. Not a word was spoken but the young farmer, Elisha, without more ado immediately followed his leader. Later, when Elijah was about to be borne away from the earth, his mantle fell upon Elisha, a symbol that he had left with him his spirit of zeal and service. All this was recognized by the sons of the prophet on the other side of the Jordan when Elisha divided the river with the same mantle, a sign that the spirit of Elijah had come upon him.

From this story, told in the fourth Book of Kings, and from the desert custom of symbolizing a contract, or compact, by the sharing of a cloak, it was plain that the Mother of God was offering her special protection to St Simon and his children. When she re-enacted the story of the garment she is alleged to have said: 'I have spread my garment over you, I have sworn a pact to you.' At the same time, she promised salvation and help to all those who called for her protection.

News of St Simon's vision spread quickly throughout Europe. So did the 'Scapular devotion', which is the wearing of small pieces from Carmelite cloaks which are blessed and regarded as a sign of Our Lady's special protection.[11] In later years Anno was to come out in defence of the traditional account although the vision of St Simon cannot be scientifically 'proved', any

---

* An account of the Carmelite Order is given in the appendix.

more than any other vision. But perhaps it is even more important to consider what the future Dr Brandsma was to call 'the foundation of the Marian character of Carmelite Spirituality'. Not only would he have read about the vision of St Simon Stock; he is certainly to have come across one of the deepest motives that makes the Carmelite link with Mary unique.

He was later to remark that the vision of the prophet Elijah on Mount Carmel requires special attention as it is the foundation of the Marian character of Carmelite Spirituality. He would refer to the fact that many commentators of scripture had seen in that little cloud that came slowly approaching from the sea and which was to deliver the parched earth by its rain a prototype of the Virgin who was to give the Redeemer. And in case his audience would find this interpretation far-fetched, Titus would remind them that more than once the presence of a cloud had been symbolic: 'In the wilderness a cloud covering the Ark of the Covenant was the sign of God's presence. Numerous instances in which this type of cloud is mentioned are applied to God's descent on earth.'

Titus would then draw attention to the circumstances in which Elijah had found himself, and which are described in 3 Kings 18, to say that 'we may conclude that to see in it a prototype of the Mother of God – a type of the mystery of the Incarnation – would be in entire agreement with the prototypal character of the Old Testament, the more so since Holy Scripture expressly mentions this vision in the life of a prophet who would be raised to such a high degree of contemplation. At all events this much is sure that within the Order the vision of Elijah has always been seen as a prototype of the mystery of Incarnation and a distant veneration of the Mother of God. And it was because of this belief, according to the tradition of Carmel, that the old sanctuary dedicated to the Holy Maid was built on the mountain in the midst of the caves. . . . We need only read the canonical hours of the feast of Our Lady of Mount Carmel to see the importance of this vision for the spiritual life of Carmel.'[12]

This was written in the thirties when Brandsma was a prominent figure at the University of Nijmegen.

Anno had discussed his impressions with some of his classmates, two of whom were to join the Carmelites at the same time. It is idle to speculate about whether Anno was instrumental in this for we can never know. All we do know is that, their studies at Megen completed, they would meet again as colleagues in Boxmeer, after a long summer holiday.

Chapter Two

NOVICE AND STUDENT

In September, 1898, Anno entered the Carmelite novitiate at
Boxmeer. The town lies beside the river Maas, half an hour's
train journey southwards from Nijmegen. Once again Anno
found himself in the province of Brabant. He was seventeen
years old, still small and slight but, with his blue eyes and dark
blond hair, quite good-looking. Although he wasn't strong, his
health was better. He had become more resilient and had
learnt to maintain his physical equilibrium.

The Carmel he entered had been founded in 1653. It was
an austere place with no time, nor inclination, for frivolity. In
the broad, flagstoned corridors hung the portraits of former
priors. Daylight entered through stained-glass windows which
depicted pious events and carried, in pompous Latin or French,
the names and titles of earlier donors. In the refectory hung
life-size portraits of former local counts and behind the desk
of the lectern a huge painting of the *Virgo Flos Carmeli* – the
Mother of Carmel. On the other walls hung a Crucifixion in
the school of van Dyck and a painting of the prophet Elijah at
the moment of his spectacular departure from the earth.

The wainscotting that ran along doors and passages and up
the stairs was heavy and dark. It could not succeed in dimming
the beautiful gate-building which connected the monastery
with the church. It was in this church, which also served as the
parish church until it was destroyed during the war, that Anno
and five others received the Carmelite habit a few days after
their arrival. From now on, he would be called by his monastic
name: Titus. He had chosen it in respect for his father and
because he knew it to have been the name of St Paul's disciple
to whom the Apostle addressed one of his letters.

Those who were Titus's companions confirm what our knowledge of him might have led us to suspect; that he set out to acquire the true Carmelite spirit with all the enthusiasm he was capable of. Life in the novitiate was not easy.

The novices were moved continually from cell to cell. The heating during the winter was totally inadequate; in fact there was only one stove in a corridor which had to do for thirteen novices in their cells.[13] As for the weather, there is, on the whole, little or no difference between the climate of Holland and that of London. When one hears people in England today remark that the pre-war winters used to start much earlier and be more severe, one would do well to remember that similar remarks are also made in Holland.

In the middle of every night the novices went to choir to recite that part of the Divine Office which is called Matins. Only when the rivers were frozen did they anticipate Matins the previous evening.[14]

The day started at 5.30 a.m. and ended at 8 p.m. It was taken up by Divine Office, Mass, meditation, spiritual reading, private study, manual labour and lectures on the Carmelite Rule and Spirituality. Those in their second year also read history and had to practise rhetoric in delivery or eloquence.

The novitiate period was reduced to one year just after Titus and his group had completed their two years – an ironic decision.

The only letter of his that has survived this period is dated October 1898, written a few weeks after he had entered Carmel. In it he wishes his mother a happy birthday and mentions that he has settled down very well. He adds that, although he has reason to think that God wants him at Carmel, he would nevertheless like them to pray for guidance as he only wants to do His will. He then reassures them again that he feels quite at home in his new life. From the beginning he had no difficulty in sleeping on a straw mattress.

A year later, on the 3rd October, Titus made his first annual profession which his parents attended. Two months later his Superior exempted him from attending Matins at night. It was evident to him that Titus was not strong enough.[15] So far, in dissertations, as well as in health, Titus had cut a poor figure.

But quite suddenly he began to improve. His finest effort was a sermon on St Titus, the text of which he kept all his life.

His novitiate was passing quickly. Forty years later someone recalled that during it he had been struck by Titus's bow and genuflection before the altar – it had totally lacked either affectation or routine formality. It was genuinely simple and reverent. His calm and absorbed posture when in prayer had already been noticed by his schoolmates at Megen and was going to impress many people from all walks of life in the years to come.

It is interesting that when witnesses of this period speak of Titus they invariably use the adjective 'ardent' to describe him.

It was in September 1900, when he was nineteen years old, that Titus began his two-year course in philosophy. Unhappily, the standard was low and the quality of teaching strangely poor. Philosophy appeared to have been treated as little more than a stepping stone to theology.

The life he was then leading certainly gave every opportunity to dig deep into the world of the Saints. It is not surprising that among his first priorities were the complete works of that remarkable woman of Avila – St Teresa – who reformed the Carmelite Order in the 16th century. The future Provincial, Dr B. Meyer, remembers that there was then a French edition by d'Andilly in the house.

The following year, 1901, Titus, then only twenty years old and a first-year student in philosophy, published an *Anthology drawn from the works of Saint Teresa*. It was the size of a prayer-book and contained three hundred and seventeen pages with a compendium of prayers which Titus added 'At request' as if the author wished to dissociate himself from those somewhat pious formulas which could never have been to his taste.

When he began his second year in philosophy, there crossed his path a man who was to exert a great influence on Titus, Doctor Hubertus Driessen.

Dr Driessen was a jovial down-to-earth man, with an abrupt manner, a business-like approach and an occasionally explosive temperament. But his laughter was as ready as his temper and he was always quick to see the point. He had been studying in Rome and was now at the age of thirty appointed to teach philosophy at Boxmeer. But his long stay at Rome had affected his Latin pronunciation to such an extent that the friars could not follow him. Consternation was universal; among some of them a stronger term would, perhaps, not have been misplaced.

Not for the last time in his life Titus acted the part of mediator. He asked for an interview with the learned doctor and, as tactfully as possible, explained the awkward situation. Would it, he suggested, be a good idea if he made some brief notes which he would like to put before Dr Hubertus for correction? Afterwards he could make copies and distribute them among his fellow students. To this Dr Hubertus replied that he would really rather write out his own lectures which he would hand to Titus who could go ahead with copying them out. This is what actually happened and as a result the master got to know his pupil better.

'I was still young and stubborn,' Titus later remarked, 'and I had my own, sometimes very pronounced, opinions about things,'[16] at which Dr Hubertus would sometimes laugh aloud.

It was the custom in the Dutch Carmelite Province that wherever a jubilee occurred, friends would contribute by writing in the *Album Amicorum*. Many years later Dr Hubertus was to write in the album that was going to be presented to Titus: 'Such readiness to be of help to others made a deep impression on me and not only on me but on all who had contacts with you.'[17] He had clearly decided to overlook his first introduction to Titus's offer of help.

The first term was hardly over when, towards the end of December, Titus's health suffered a serious set-back. He had a haemorrhage which was thought to have been caused by his old stomach weakness. For many weeks he was confined to his cell and forbidden to study. The Prior saw to it that everything was done for his recovery. He was allowed the odd visitor who would always be welcomed by a broad smile.[18] Dr Hubertus, too, made an occasional appearance but was told to keep off the subject of philosophy.

Titus recalled these visits many years later in the 'Album' presented to Dr Hubertus on the occasion of his golden jubilee. It is one of the rare autobiographical notes Titus has given us.

'In those brief moments,' he wrote, 'you told me now this and then that about your Roman days, about your trials and difficulties, about your occasionally bold opposition to what you thought to be wrong – not to make me bitter or critical, that you never did, but to make me see that something had to be done and could be done.'

It was an important stage in Titus's life. He was growing up. During these visits, he became aware that he was a member of a world-wide family of Carmelites. And he began to realize, too, that, as in all families, there were conflicting views and tendencies at work between various members of it, that not everyone in the Order agreed about the role it should play in the future. After these brief visits he thought about it a great deal.

'There is always a turning point,' he wrote. 'The Lord does not wish things to remain always the same. There are moments in time when people must come forward who are willing and able to change them, not in a spirit of rebellion but from a genuine love of the Order and its continued development.'

We know that the thought about 'God's plan with us' frequently preoccupied him in later days.

Already it must have been pretty obvious to him, as it is to us now, that Dr Hubertus's words to him were not merely academic, the overflow of his own concern, but that he already saw in Titus a disciple of the future – one who would help to bring about the turning point.

Soon he was to know. But for the time being, he must concentrate on getting well. He was already much better. At last he was allowed to resume his studies, to work hard again in an effort to catch up with the others. In this he succeeded and was ready in time to take and pass his final exams.

Chapter Three

DR EUGENIUS

Titus had spent four years at Boxmeer when he and the students of his year left in September 1902 for Zenderen to begin their four-year course in theology.

It was here, not long afterwards, that Dr Hubertus dropped in on him to tell him that the Provincial, who resided at Zenderen, had just informed him that he had been nominated Procurator of the entire Order. It meant, of course, that he would have to return to Rome.

'I was delighted,' Titus reminisces in the album. 'I did not share your objection about being too young. I was twenty-two and although you were thirty-two I looked up to you as a man of experience. I thought you should certainly go; that way you could do a great deal for the well-being of the whole Order.'

Before parting, Dr Hubertus suggested that Titus might keep their ideas alive among his companions and should occasionally send him a line to keep him in touch.

The first year in theology passed quietly. Zenderen was quite different from Boxmeer. To begin with, the Priory was situated in a small village in a much more Protestant part of the country. The Carmelites there ran their own junior seminary; they went out to assist in the neighbouring parishes while the secular priests often came in to make their retreat. The whole environment was much more fluid and relaxed. It was quite a different atmosphere from that of the novitiate house.

Once the first year of theology was over, the student-friars went to Oss, in the province of Brabant, to complete the remaining three years of the course. Here at Oss they were to have as their teacher and Prefect of Studies another Driessen: Dr Eugenius Driessen, brother of Dr Hubertus.

Dr Eugenius, who was five years older than his brother, was a very learned man and enjoyed a high reputation. But he did not carry his learning lightly. His lectures were dull and unimaginative. Not only did he not encourage free and open discussion about theological issues, he regarded it as a dangerous indication of unorthodoxy. He did not take kindly, therefore, to a student who queried the theological position. In this aspect he differed altogether from his brother Hubertus, though it should be remembered that the latter was a philosopher and that any original theological thinking was quickly suspect in those days.

As Titus had a questioning mind and did not hide this side of his character, it was inevitable that Dr Eugenius should view his pupil with a certain amount of suspicion. A slight tension became noticeable in the classroom whenever Titus put up his hand and questioned what was, to Dr Eugenius, 'sacrosanct'.

Reminiscing on those hours in the classroom, Titus was later to comment: 'I am afraid I was rather conceited in those days.' [19]

His classmates, however, don't go along with this self-confession. As soon as Dr Eugenius had shown that he wouldn't have any more contradiction, Titus, they said, would remain absolutely silent. But we all know that silence is often a most effective weapon and Dr Eugenius knew very well, as he once admitted, that their views on certain matters were totally opposed. He, therefore, could not be expected to suggest or to support the idea of a teaching career for Titus within the Order.

One must not, however, over-dramatize the issue although later, at the time of Titus's final examinations, there would occur one moment of real drama. But apart from this, their personal relationship was good, and it was equally with Dr Eugenius's full approval and support that Titus was allowed to start an academic society as well as a House publication to stimulate ideas. In the beginning the periodical was hand-written and later stencilled in Amsterdam. From time to time a good article was forwarded to a periodical of repute and would thus reach a wider public as well as being a source of financial help to their own venture.

In one of the first articles that found its way into the world, Titus asked how many able and talented men there are hidden behind monastic walls who, in accordance with their spiritual Rule, ought to use their abilities for the well-being of humanity. He pointed out that the records show that, in earlier days, all kinds of Religious Orders were contributing to the world's progress and that it would be altogether wrong to deny them their chance today. He even referred to the *Her Katholiek Sociaal Weekblad* ('Catholic Social Weekly') which has emphasized that it was precisely these Religious Orders who were most likely and able to provide men whose dedication would be both whole-hearted and free from selfish interest.

He went even further. He quoted from authorities to support his view that, in order to exert influence, a man must conquer the right to do so; that whoever wants to reform society and contribute to the solution of its problems must first prove his credentials by becoming a competitor in the open arena of the world.

Titus had now begun to disseminate the ideas that he shared with Dr Hubertus in Rome through his monthly publication. By this, as well as by means of the academic society in the house, he hoped to stimulate thought and raise the standard of discussion. He was convinced that not only does it not run contrary to the Carmelite Rule that its members should engage in apostolic activity but that it is in fact their duty to do so as effectively as possible. But he was careful not to lose sight of the other side of his vocation in his enthusiasm. Many years later (when speaking in English at the University of Washington) he reminded his audience that the Carmelites consider themselves the privileged children of the great prophet and ask from him 'the portion of the first born'.

'But only he who has the intention of maintaining the noble tradition of the House may ask this privileged portion. ... Elijah was, above all, the great contemplative; but God called him many times from his contemplation to the active life, and his place in the history of Israel is as one of its most untiring labourers. He always returned to the solitude of the life of contemplation. So the Carmelites must be contemplatives who from their active life always return to the contemplation as to the higher and better part of their vocation.'[20]

It was part of the mystery of his personality that Titus was able to know so whole-heartedly the practical and pragmatic world of spending while preserving himself within the Carmelite rule of being closely united to God in prayer.

The House publication was so well received that, after two years, Titus could get it printed. Other members of the Community then took over the editorship with Titus as secretary, for it had been decided that it should become a periodical for the whole of the Dutch Carmelite Province. If hitherto it had been named after the great Carmelite, Baptista Mantuanus, now it was to appear under the unassuming name of *Van Neerlands Carmel* ('from the Dutch Carmel').

Later, with Titus' departure from Oss, the publication was to go downhill and it pained him that it eventually ceased altogether. But even though his own style improved as the magazine grew, one cannot, in all honesty, say that he was himself a great stylist. In his schooldays he had written some verses and poetry. But this was no more than a lip service to the current practice of the day. Nevertheless, in content and argument, his own articles were among the best that were published.

On the 17th June, 1905, seven years after he had entered Carmel, Titus and his confrères were ordained to the priesthood in the Cathedral at Den Bosch. He was twenty-four years old. Afterwards they all went home to celebrate their first solemn Mass and were given ten days off. But they were not at the end of their course. As they had been ordained at the end of their third year in theology they still had one more year to do.

It was generally accepted that Titus was destined for Higher Studies at the Gregorian University in Rome. There was, however, one man who disagreed with this view. It will come as no surprise to the reader to learn that this man was Dr Eugenius. Unfortunately his vote was, as it turned out, crucial. For not only was he a highly esteemed Prefect of Studies but also Titus's teacher and examiner.

When the day of the final examination arrived, Titus saw that he had been asked to defend a thesis concerning the Essence of Angels. At this most critical moment Titus asked if he might be permitted to act as prosecuting, instead of defence, counsel and to argue the opposite case to that proposed by the thesis. There was a stunned pause. Dr Eugenius's subsequent indignation was due perhaps less to the nature of the argument than Titus's audacious request. To him it seemed an act of gross impertinence. To the council that was to decide the future of the candidates Dr Eugenius pointed out it would be dangerous and unsuitable to allow such a man to teach. His view was upheld and the future of Titus, or so it seemed, was settled.

In fairness to Dr Eugenius, it should, perhaps, be pointed out that Titus had not been asked for a profession of his personal faith when he was asked to discuss and defend a thesis concerning the Essence of Angels. He had been asked for an academic answer to an academic question. With another more imaginative or humorous examiner, he might have got away with it, especially if his performance had justified his request. But he knew his tutor. It was an indescribably foolish thing to have done – to have tweaked the tail of the tiger.

Perhaps, in the cold light of subsequent events, he realized this. At any rate, he made no complaint when he learnt his fate. He was appointed sacristan and financial administrator of the Church's finances. The decision must have hurt unbearably. But to no one did he grumble or show the depth of his disappointment.

While Dr Hubertus in Rome learnt with stupefaction and annoyance of the decision that Titus was considered too dangerous and unreliable to be allowed to teach, Titus himself got down to his new duties with as much goodwill as he could muster. They included occasionally assisting in neighbouring parishes and, mercifully, he was still able to carry on with the publication of the magazine.

In a sense it was as much a setback for Dr Hubertus as it was for Titus, for it was he who had helped to make him what he was; he who was, in a sense, responsible for the views that Titus held. But for the moment there was little he could do. It was no time for action (even if any had been possible) when feelings ran high and the gates of negotiation were firmly closed. But none of the three main characters involved could have remained unaware of the irony of their situation – locked, like a Greek tragedy, in a triangular maze of circumstances from which, it seemed at the time, there was no possible way out.

Chapter Four

STUDENT-PRIEST AT ROME

But fate, or God, was on Titus's side. Towards the end of September, or beginning of October, an illness in the Driessen family led to Dr Hubertus's recall from Rome. Hardly had he arrived in Holland to visit his family when he headed straight for Oss. Titus wisely kept silent and out of the way. Father Hubertus did not. If his brother's fame and position within the Dutch Province had strongly influenced the decision about Titus, Dr Hubertus's own fame and position which extended to the whole Order was about to tip the scales. For he demanded no less than a reconsideration of the case of Titus Brandsma. During the special meeting of the Chapter that was called, the Procurator-General succeeded in breaking down the opposition. A few days later Titus appeared at Zenderen for a private talk with the Provincial.

To others, later, he reported that during it he spoke with great frankness, making no attempt to conceal his views. He had even gone so far as to remind the Provincial that Dr Eugenius regarded him as potentially dangerous and that it was quite true that he had felt unable to swallow several of the scholastic arguments put to him; he also wanted the Provincial to understand that he would not be able to expect others to accept everything they were told blindly, any more than he did himself. When he remarked: 'You know what an independent mind I have', the Provincial had· interrupted. 'That,' he is said to have replied, 'is precisely why you should go to Rome, so that you can study philosophy better.'[21]

Not long afterwards, relieved and thankful, Dr Hubertus and Titus travelled together to Rome. They visited Cologne, stayed with the Carmelites at Mainburg in Bavaria and broke their journey in pink-marbled Verona. They arrived, in the pouring rain, in Rome on the 31st of October.[22]

The Carmelite House, 'Collegio San Alberto', lies close to St Peter's.[23] There Titus was to meet a mixed community from all over the world, Italians, Spanish, Maltese, Sicilians, Bavarians, Austrians and Irish. Titus's former Prior at Boxmeer, Gabriel Wessels, was also at Rome. It was good to see him. Both Gabriel Wessels and Dr Hubertus were anxious that Titus should receive special attention in regard to his meals as they feared that the Italian diet of the house might prove inadequate for him.[24] Both had vivid memories of Titus's illness when he was a student in philosophy, and they knew how hard Roman conditions can weigh upon men from northern countries who are not used to pasta and the charms of a farinaceous menu.

Their day began at 5.15 a.m. and ended at 10 p.m. Four times a day Titus was to cross the Ponte Sant'Angelo bridge to attend courses at the Gregorian University. During the three-year course he had undertaken it was not only speculative philosophy that he had to study but also experimental physics to which geometry, mathematics, physiology and astronomy belonged. But it was not enough. There was something else he very much wanted to do.

Half reluctantly Dr Hubertus gave in to Titus's plea to be allowed to go twice a week to the Leonine Institute where Pottier, whose reputation was high, was giving a course in sociology. At Oss, Titus had met Mr P. J. M. Aalberse, the future Dutch Minister of Social Affairs, and he had subsequently contributed to his paper by writing an article about the rôle of a priest in social life. From Rome he would now and then be able to send back an article. But he would play it down to his Superiors who were afraid that he was taking on too much, and assure them that he wrote these articles more or less by chance.[25] He was restless in his desire to get things done, anxious to put into practice his views about the rôle of a modern priest. He got in touch with the leaders of the Italian Catholic Social Action, convinced that no sphere of human life should remain alienated from the Christian influence if men were ever going to be brought to live in union with God.

One day he went, with Dr Hubertus, to see Pope Pius X, the barefooted boy from the Venetian district who had always loved evangelical simplicity and portrayed it in his life as curate, parish priest, bishop and patriarch, and who had every intention of living up to it as Pope, which he was from 1903 to 1914. He brought down the accustomed age for children making their first Holy Communion and each Sunday gave 'Sunday Class' to the people of Rome. The letters Titus sent home reveal that ·he was particularly impressed by the Pope's face. Dr Hubertus and he were in a group audience at the time and when the Pope reached the two Carmelites he was heard to say: 'Ah, patres nostri,' apparently referring to the days when he was Bishop in Mantua where the Carmelites had a house.[26] It was a comforting and endearing phrase.

Like many others before and after him, Titus fell in love with Rome. He enjoyed every aspect of it. For a certain period Titus celebrated each Sunday morning Mass in the private chapel of a Roman princess. At home he joined whenever possible in the Choir recitation of the Divine Office. But at the end of his first academic year, when the summer heat scourged Rome, Dr Hubertus took him away from San Alberto to their house in Vienna where the air was cooler and it was possible to breathe and think. It was not a moment too soon, for Titus's health was giving some cause for concern.

The two Carmelites were particularly interested in seeing for themselves the social conditions in Vienna, and together they later wrote an article about their impressions.

From Vienna they went on to Straubing in Bavaria where Titus, suffering from blood-poisoning, ran a high temperature and had to be fed through a tube. However, undeterred by the prospect of more travelling, he was sufficiently well after a few days to go on to their house at Mainburg where they had stayed on their way to Rome the previous year. There, Titus convalesced and followed the Carmelite Rule of Life. Presumably the budget could not run to the two of them to travelling all the way back to Holland.

Titus was to spend the summer months at Mainburg again the following year by which time he had acquired his teaching licence. He still had another year to do before he could take his doctorate. In the autumn of that final year, Dr Hubertus' term of office as Procurator-General was over and he returned to Holland. It is possible that the latter's departure meant a relaxation in watchfulness over Titus's health, for during the winter months he suffered a haemorrhage and was for a long time gravely ill. They even feared for his life. One of his Italian companions at San Alberto by the name of Gramatico, who in later years was to become Assistant General in the Order, had become one of Titus's best friends. He visited him regularly and claimed that Titus suffered bravely and cheerfully. The two used to converse in a mixture of Latin and Italian.

Titus's convalescence was slow and, as a result, he lost several months of valuable studies. Though well aware that the hour of his final examinations was rapidly approaching, it would be to misunderstand Titus to think of him as having been tense, depressed, or worried. Resignation and confidence were two striking characteristics of him while his inner peace and cheerfulness seemed untouchable. The reader saw this first illustrated during Titus's illness as a student in Boxmeer and later again when his road to higher studies seemed barred by Dr Eugenius.

Because he lost the great part of his academic year, the authorities at the Gregorian University at first refused point blank to allow him permission to sit for the examinations. But his pleading was, as usual, effective and he won the day. But not the accolade; the examiners had been right. The gap proved too wide and Titus failed. 'It had to be that way,' he wrote to Dr Hubertus, 'I am very sorry, but at any rate I am quite well.' [27] He had had an earlier and harsher lesson in how to accept disappointment. It stood him in good stead now.

When Dr Hubertus learnt the whole story behind the failure, the months of illness and slow convalescence, he was extremely worried. He didn't trust Titus a minute longer in Rome, and wrote to tell him to get on the next train to Holland. But this advice was easier to give than to receive. Titus replied that it just wasn't possible, but he would return in a week.

Meanwhile, he had also received his nomination as teacher in philosophy at the Carmelite House in Oss. The Provincial

Chapter had apparently taken this decision irrespective of the result of Titus's exams. It was not dependent upon his getting his doctor's degree. On the 2nd of June he said Mass at the old Carmelite Church in Genoa and continued his journey home from there via Geneva and Freibourg. His health was better and during the rest of the summer he studied a great deal with the intention of sitting for his finals once again that autumn.

Early in October he returned to Rome where, on the 25th of that month, he received his doctorate. He was twenty-eight years old.

PART TWO

The Years of Achievement

Chapter Five

PROFESSOR AND JOURNALIST
(1909–23)

〜〜〜〜〜〜〜〜〜〜〜〜〜〜〜〜〜〜〜〜〜〜〜〜〜〜〜〜〜

Titus was to lecture at Oss for the next fourteen years. He was fortunate in having been away for he came back with a new perspective. During the two years that they both had been in Rome, Dr Hubertus had kept Titus fully informed about the ups and downs in the Carmel Order and, after his departure, others had seen to it that Titus was kept in touch with fresh developments. Both men were deeply dedicated to their vocation in the Order and especially to the Dutch branch of it.

Titus was to return to Holland at a critical moment in the development of the Dutch Carmel. A Chapter was just about to be held and Rome had designated Dr Hubertus to preside over it. Due to the fact that Dr Hubertus was residing at some distance from him in Zenderen we have a couple of letters which Titus sent to him from Oss. They are concerned with only one thing: will the Chapter support their ideals? Will a strong leader emerge as Provincial? Will he gain support for a central house of studies? What will be done about the Brazilian mission? 'Let us hope and pray,' Titus added anxiously to one of his letters.

The opening speech of the Chapter was to be given by Dr Hubertus himself. The text was sent to Titus. What did he think of it? He replied with the same frankness that must have comforted as well as unsettled the Provincial who had interviewed him in Zenderen three years before.

'I have only one criticism to make about its conclusion,' Titus replied, and in his reply the characters of both men are clearly shown. Titus might have been the older writing to the younger man. 'And you yourself have already mentioned that you were thinking of altering it. . . . Please, in God's name, read it slowly, slowly, slowly. Otherwise you may as well stay away. . . . You have in most instances spoken as from my own heart – solidly, persuasively and out of love for the growth of the Order [as well as] impartially . . . considering the circumstances but it is somewhat too strongly worded, too personal.'

Titus was afraid of an unfavourable impression. He therefore advised Dr Hubertus not to speak over-drastically, of 'a matter of life or death'.

'Say rather that they should carefully consider what it is that may advance Carmel or may lead to its ruin, and that they should unhesitatingly vote for one who, in these times, appears to be the most suitable person to help us advance, not merely to guide, but to advance. Make a simple, brief, businesslike, calm and especially impersonal ending. . . . Don't be sharp . . . remain calm and stick to the point. Respect as much as possible the opinion of others . . . don't attack them.'[28]

He waited anxiously for the result of both his letter and of Dr Hubertus's speech. In the morning of the 24th August, Titus received the news that Dr Hubertus had been chosen as the next Provincial, a position he was going to hold for the following six years. The Chapter that had elected him remained in session and supported the motion for setting up a central House of Studies – a decision long awaited by both Dr Hubertus and Titus. It was a moment of triumph, although, for the time being, this new foundation had to remain seriously understaffed. Titus had suggested to Dr Hubertus several names of potential professors who might be considered for a university training and he was careful to keep his friends in Rome in touch with their progress.

In September Titus began to teach philosophy. He had a class of twelve. In this, had he known it, he should have counted himself lucky. The following year there were to be no students at all. For Titus it would be a chance to strengthen the understaffed team of theology professors and to catch up on his spiritual reading. But it was sad all the same. These were the years just before the First World War when the Religious Orders did not get many candidates. The Carmelites were not well known and it sometimes happened, as it did now, that there were years without a single novice.

The end of the First World War was to effect a marked change. Perhaps the fact of suffering had made men once more susceptible to contemplation. At any rate Carmel was to benefit from a large increase in vocations. But, in 1909, this still lay in the future. Nothing was certain and Dr Hubertus's and Titus's confidence in planning a central House of Studies and raising the standard much higher was both courageous and, as it turned out, perceptive.

Titus appeared unaffected by the small size of his class. He gave himself no less conscientiously in his attempt to link the philosophical aspect of an issue with the theological so that his students should grasp the idea that things should be seen in the round, in their entirety. During these years Titus was able to deepen his knowledge of mysticism though he did not do so at the expense of his life. When he had barely reached the required minimum age of thirty he was made a member of the Definitory – a consultative body with voting powers which assisted the Provincial in conducting the affairs of the Carmelite Province. These members were elected by the professed members of the various Houses in the Province. For three years Titus was a member of the Definitory, and after a gap of another three years he returned to it for the remaining days of his life.

Apart from his teaching and the growing journalistic ventures (which we are about to consider), he was continually asked to start, or carry through, a series of different things. His efficiency, as well as his tact, grew with the years, while they melted imperceptibly into each other. To be born with the desire to write is to be born with a restless spirit that can only be temporarily assuaged when the pen is in one's hand. It is not necessary to succeed, or to be good at it. To write is, for many, its own reward.

To Titus, in spite of a style that remained mediocre, it was the natural way of expressing his apostolic ambitions. Instinctively, at moments of crisis or conviction, he reached for his pen. And during the years he was at Oss (1909–23) he reached for it more and more frequently.

At first, like many writers, his goal exceeded his grasp. We know, for instance, that he had discussed a plan for a national paper with Mr Aalberse who edited a paper on social questions.[29] But the idea was not encouraged although it would have embodied all his ideas about priests and their relations with the world at large. Titus felt even more strongly, perhaps, about a Carmelite publication. To him it seemed indispensable for the Order's growth and impact. But of all his great plans it was the least ambitious which was to be realized. *Carmelrozen*, as it came to be called, was to concentrate on making Carmel known to the general public.

One Saturday morning in November, 1911, Titus travelled to Boxmeer to discuss the typography and layout. Somewhat laboriously he explained what he had in mind. But fate was now to intervene. It so happened that one of his colleagues began to spread stories in Boxmeer about the Provincial's views on the venture and while this colleague was in Zenderen, where the Provincial resided, he did the same about Titus. To make matters worse, the Provincial, Dr Hubertus, had just received a letter from Titus in which the latter candidly stated that, in his study of the German philosopher, Immanuel Kant, Hubertus had been too sharp in his criticism. When, therefore, the rumours reached the Provincial, he exploded and wrote a strongly-worded letter to Titus.

The whole incident pained Titus. He simply replied that all he had aimed at was to find a happy medium between the idealistic and material side of the venture. Surely Hubertus didn't wish it to become merely a source of income. Furthermore, he succeeded in getting to the bottom of the affair by discovering who had been twisting the truth. But this was an empty discovery for the incident still left its mark. It was probably responsible for Titus's failing to become the editor. He did, however, sit on the editorial board and became, in effect, the *eminence grise* behind the whole venture. He wrote countless articles and worked unceasingly in its regard. And after one year of publication there were already eleven thousand subscribers, which was not bad for a novice in journalism.

Carmelrozen was dedicated to the Mother of God. Not surprisingly, some of the best articles are those written about her in her relation to the Son of God as well as to the sons of men. Throughout, Titus was careful to avoid sentimentality, but his personal devotion shines through all the same.

'The mystery of the Incarnation,' he once wrote, 'has revealed to us how valuable man is to God, how intimately God wants to be united to man. This wonder draws one's attention to the eternal birth of the Son from the Father as the deepest reason for this mystery of love. In the celebration of the three Masses at Christmas, the birth from the Father is first celebrated; secondly, from the Virgin Mary; thirdly, God's birth in ourselves. This is not done without significance and this threefold birth must be understood to be a revelation of one eternal love . . . we should always remember the threefold birth as phases of one great process of love. . . . The contemplation of this mystery has led to a twofold devotion to Mary, which we had better describe as an imitation, gradually deepening into a close union with her. One should not think of the imitation without thinking of the union nor of the union without the thought of the imitation.'[30]

Again, elsewhere, when referring to her title *Theotokos* ('Godbearer') which the Council of Ephesus bestowed on her and which best describes her place in the mystery of Salvation, Titus wrote: 'It is our calling to be, after her, *Theotokos*, Godbearers in the world.'

He suggested that her image should have a place in every room 'just because we are human and nourish the mind through the senses.' He himself, as one of the photographs shows, kept a statue of her on his desk. And, in the years to come, when he was imprisoned by the Nazis, he tore a picture of her out of his breviary so that he could see her each day 'first and last'.

In 1916, Titus began to think of extending his early work on St Teresa. The following year he put his plan before a publisher: nothing less than a translation into Dutch of the complete works of Teresa of Avila. It numbered seven volumes. But he was not alone in this enterprise. His collaborators were to be Dr Athanasius van Rijswijck, who taught Church history, and the two brothers, Hubertus and Eugenius Driessen. These men were regarded as the ablest men in the Dutch Province. Together they formed a team and shared out the works to be translated. The organization rested with Titus, who was also to see to the correction of the page-proofs and to be responsible for the correlation of the footnotes.

The first publication, Teresa's biography, was Titus's effort alone. It appeared in 1918 and was very well received. Not unreasonably the publishers pressed for the rest. When this team of four first undertook the task they had been confident that they could meet the challenge. But the reorganization of the Carmelite studies at home and in their Brazilian mission, the departure of Dr Eugenius Driessen to Rome, the newly-acquired mission in the Dutch East Indies, and the appointment of Titus to the University of Nijmegen had resulted in heavy demands on each in turn so that they could no longer cope with this particular venture.

By 1936 four parts had come from the press. But others were to finish the remaining three volumes after the war.[31] It was also at this period that Titus got himself heavily involved in the Frisian cause. His Superiors allowed him to join a team of Frisian Catholics who had many contacts and enjoyed working with non-Catholics in the common objective. Perhaps it was through this that he met the man with whom he was to arrange a Frisian version of the *Imitation of Christ*.[32] For this, too, was a combined effort between Titus and a non-Catholic. While the Frisian movement was, in fact, a cultural movement which aimed at recognition of the Frisian language, a reawakening of awareness of the religious and historical aspect of Frisian life, it roused a certain amount of suspicion and resentment. There were some who saw in it a movement with separatist tendencies. But luckily Titus was able to take steps to allay these fears in time.

His correspondence grew hugely in line with his growing commitments. It is, therefore, a little surprising that Dr Hubertus, who was always so anxious about Titus's health and constantly afraid that he would undertake too much, took him one spring morning in 1919 to the publisher of the local paper at Oss which resulted in his appointment as editor of that paper.

The state of the paper had been steadily growing worse; sometimes it had only two pages, at times it did not appear at all. Probably Dr Hubertus felt that Titus alone could save it. If so, he was right. Titus formed a team of contributors chosen from Carmel as well as from outside. Before long the paper appeared regularly twice a week; on Saturdays it had eight pages to its credit.

It was an intensely busy period for Titus. For, out of the blue, he had suddenly to step in as Head of the recently-opened Lycée. This was a Carmelite foundation where, as it happened, he was to remain for several weeks.

We know that, at this period, Titus was still at his desk at half-past one in the morning, although at 6.30 a.m. he would be at the altar saying Mass and at 8 o'clock in school.[33] More than once he was accused of dissipating his energies though he always seemed the right man for each job.

It is generally through his active life that we shall catch an occasional glimpse of his soul, for he never spoke of his inner life. At the time he came, perhaps, nearest to what we consider to be the ideal combination of the contemplative and the active life. For, as he once said, 'Inevitably, in almost all circumstances of modern life, the active apostolate makes its great demands on Carmel. This activity must be rooted in contemplation, since it is its only source and warrant of fruitfulness.

'There have been times, especially in the first centuries of the establishment of the Order in the West, when urgent needs of the Church were neglected for the sake of the contemplative ideal. At other times the spirit of contemplation has been lost in too great activity. The combination of these two lives has presented a difficult problem even to St Teresa, who in her reform finds it difficult to draw a dividing line.'[34]

From his Carmelite life at Oss, where he still taught philosophy to a small class of students, he had embraced the Frisian cause, inaugurated a Carmelite publication, undertaken the translation of the works of St Teresa of Avila with a specially selected team, taken charge of the local paper and been re-elected a member of the Definitory.

Where was he personally to draw the line? Quite clearly his own Superiors, who were so concerned about him, did not know the answer except that, to Titus' regret, they forbade him to join the Community so early in the morning for the recitation of the Divine Office.

In the same year as his appointment as editor of the local paper (1919) Titus was approached by the local Dean about the prospect of a library. He accepted the challenge and succeeded in obtaining financial support from the Ministry in The Hague as well as from local bodies and industries. Once everything was under way, he handed it over to one of his colleagues at Carmel to run. He was becoming an expert in the art of delegation (although he continued to take great interest in this project) as well as in the art of initiation.

Shortly after the 1914 war, the missionary spirit seized the imagination of the Dutch. During the summer of 1919, Titus himself was appointed to teach in Brazil, in the actual mission whose future had so much interested him when he arrived at Oss ten years before. The Provincial had, however, second thoughts about the matter. Perhaps he realized that Titus's departure for Brazil would have seriously impeded the building up of Carmel at home.

The Provincial at this time was Cyprianus Verbeek, a wise and gentle man who held the rare distinction of being twice re-elected to the post. In that capacity he was Titus's Superior from 1921 to 1930. Titus felt that he had somehow to contribute something to the missions, and so, during the summer of 1921, he travelled around the country with a projector and slides, hoping to arouse interest in the missions. Having thus spent a whole week in the town of Goes, he went off to Boxmeer to make a similar effort while the first Mission Congress at Maastricht awaited him a few days later. Titus' efforts proved too much. At Boxmeer he fell ill.

As it so happened, this coincided with a visit from his mother who had come up to see him that warm Sunday, the 3rd July. The previous year her husband had died and Titus had been absolutely wonderful to his dying father and of great comfort to his mother.[35] She was now travelling around Holland, visiting all her children. Arriving at Boxmeer she found her son quite exhausted and looking ill and decided to take him back to his Priory at Oss. Ironically, once there, the monastic Rule prevented her from entering the enclosure. But knowing that her son would be well looked after she left him and returned home.

It must have comforted Titus to know that his mother would not˙ be returning to an empty farmhouse in Friesland. His parents had retired several years before to a small easily-run house in Bolsward which lay close to the farm which had then been taken over by their married daughter, Gatske.

That same day Titus had a serious haemorrhage. For several weeks he was gravely ill and the students kept a round-the-clock watch on him. It was in moments like these that he made such an impression on those around him. He was cheerful, resigned and grateful for every attention he received. Once more he recovered. Needless to say he was told to curb his appetite for work. It was not until November that the doctors discharged their patient, four months after he had fallen ill.

He was overjoyed to read in the newspapers that, throughout the country, the halls were packed with people who had come in support of the missions. At the same time his own efforts for a grand Mission Week at Oss turned out a splendid success. Shortly afterwards, the anxiously awaited news came from Rome entrusting half the Vicariat of Java, an area of five million inhabitants, to the care of the Dutch Carmelite Province. Titus was clearly moved.

During the years that Dr Hubertus had been Provincial and had taken up residence at Oss, the two could regularly be seen walking together, their heads bowed in absorbed conversation, or argument, engrossed in the running of a growing Order and an expanding mission. Now Dr Hubertus was once again Procurator-General in Rome and Titus wrote to him: 'We are hard-pressed'; and by this he meant in manpower as well as financially. In answer, he learnt that the General of the Order wanted two very able professors from Holland in 'San Alberto' which was getting ready to become the Carmelites' International College in Rome.

Inevitably Titus was to be one of them. To this he replied
that he was quite indifferent to his personal fate, the vow of
obedience solving all that. He was ready to leave any day,
whether it be for Australia, Japan, Russia, or America, and he
added that his health was quite good.[36] Meanwhile, wisely, he
went on with his work as if nothing would happen. Nothing in
fact did happen.

During all these moves it would be wrong to think that Titus
remained aloof from his fellow men. He was a warm-hearted
champion who would go to any lengths to support someone
whose cause he had adopted, as the case of Albert Servaes
showed.

Albert Servaes was an artist who had painted a startling set
of Stations of the Cross for a lonely chapel in Belgium which
had caused an immediate public outcry. Titus took Servaes's
case so much to heart that he sent letters and telegrams to Dr
Hubertus in Rome pleading with him to discuss the affair with
the General of the Religious Order to which the Rector of the
Chapel belonged. (It was this General who had ordered the
Rector to remove the Stations from the Chapel.) Titus's efforts
were in vain. The General abided by his decision. Distressed
and humiliated by the publicity they had received, both the
Rector and artist turned to Titus for help. Their reputations
were at stake.

Before long, and to the general surprise of the public, a
well-known magazine reproduced illustrations of Servaes's
Stations of the Cross, accompanied by a commentary and a
meditation for each Station from the pen of Titus Brandsma.
It was a tactful plea for understanding for the modern vision
of Servaes's religious paintings.

This was Titus's first major public appearance as a conciliator.
Servaes, however, was not the only artist that Titus became
involved with. The sculptor, Auguste Falise, was also to
experience his help.

Falise was a highly emotional man and financially in low
water. Titus had been instrumental in getting him the commission of sculpting a statue of Christ-the-King for the town of Oss.
But Falise's work had met with a dubious reception. The

criticism affected him deeply. Once more it was up to Titus to cheer him up. He tried to find other commissions for him and even obtained a decoration for Falise which would give him some public recognition. He also went out of his way to find employment for Falise's son-in-law and, later on, found him a house.

In fact, there were few lengths to which Titus would not go for those in any sort of trouble, often without reward or recognition. But not in the case of Falise, for he was one of those rare men who find it easy to receive gracefully. A footnote to one of his letters reads, like a prayer in reverse: 'Indispensable Titus, God bless you.'

Chapter Six

THE YEARS AT NIJMEGEN

~~~~~~

Towards the end of April, 1923, Titus received a telegram asking him to see Professor Dr Hoogveld. Mystified by the summons, he nevertheless obeyed it. So he was to learn that the Archbishop of Utrecht, encouraged by the financial response of the Dutch Catholics, had decided to start a Catholic University at Nijmegen. For no substantial reason one of the Ministers in The Hague had opposed the appointment of Dr Ferdinand Sassen[37] (who at a later stage was appointed) to the Chair of Philosophy. It was then that someone had proposed Dr Titus Brandsma. Would he accept?

On an earlier occasion, Dr Hoogveld had mentioned to Titus that the subject of 'mysticism' would be placed on the agenda of the future University. Titus had taken it as a hint. Actually, when, in response to the telegram, he went to the meeting he was told that he would be required to share the Chair of Philosophy with Dr Hoogveld while 'mysticism' was to go to a Dominican. Without revealing his own views, Titus forwarded the confidential message to Dr Hubertus in Rome. On the evening of the 27th June, the Provincial officially announced the news of Titus' appointment in the refectory at Oss. The annals of Carmel read: *Omnes gaudio implevit* ('everyone was delighted'). They could not know that Titus would remain there for nineteen years of his life.

He was to teach the history of philosophy except that of the Greeks and Romans, natural philosophy, natural theology, the philosophy of history, and, furthermore, the history of mysticism with a special emphasis on Dutch mysticism.[38] Five months after the idea was first mentioned, he moved in September to Nijmegen where he was given a house[39] in which he was to

56

occupy a large suite with a sideroom and balcony. Behind the house there was a garden where he was frequently to be seen with his breviary or rosary. Unfortunately the premises no longer exist. They were destroyed during the war in September 1944.

At first he used to say how pleased he was at the prospect of devoting himself completely to study but, of course, his apostolic character would never allow itself to be totally suppressed and it would be active again. In October the University opened. It had yet to prove itself. Among the first students who came there was one who recalled that Professor Brandsma did not (like the other professors) head straight for the rostrum but went instead to meet and welcome the newcomers. No one knew Professor Brandsma, but he lost no time in introducing himself to them with his usual mixture of tact and kindness. During the first few years he was to study hard from early morning until late at night. He enjoyed the opportunity of adding to his already well-stocked mind. As he said later to one of his students: 'I learned an enormous lot at Nijmegen.'[40]

Certainly all his philosophy books, from Boethius to Bergson and Husserl, were so well handled that soon they looked very shabby because Titus read them while travelling from place to place on his university and non-university missions. The subjects he had to teach were in the nature of a makeshift. Secretly, no doubt, he would have preferred to teach mysticism for it was a subject very close to his heart. At any rate, it held greater interest for him than philosophy, in which Dr Hoogveld was to excel.

Perhaps that is why his lectures on philosophy lacked at times the clarity and interest of his others. Some of his early philosophical students remarked that although he could develop a personal vision with great lucidity, he was sometimes difficult to follow. Some were even rather bored. But, as a pupil said, if one could get through the early stages one was all right. It was worth persevering, and they took care not to miss his classes.

In the history faculty the main theme of his lectures was the divine pattern to be seen in human events; in the years 1934 and 1935 he produced an admirable development of *lex domini in historia*.

On philosophical matters, however, he wrote little. He waited in vain for the 'quiet months' he had envisaged which would have given him the opportunity. But here and there among his works we come across a well-expressed thought or a vigorous reflection on the subject.

He was a better thinker than he was a speaker, entirely free of affectation or pomposity, a man to whom dogmatism and intolerance were both completely alien. Perhaps this is why, when faced with those young men who required, as Montaigne said, a head to be well-formed rather than well-filled, he considered it his first duty to love them in order to understand them. Certainly he did his best to get to know them. He tried equally hard to captivate them but he knew that he lacked the rhetorical gift of some of his colleagues. Extempore speech was never his strong point, so he made up by preparing his subject matter with care. The modulations of his voice, the gestures of his well-made hands, and the vivacity of his eyes managed to get across to his audience thoughts which had a resolute, worthwhile quality and often turned out to be far more interesting than his students had expected.

Gradually it became clear that he himself was loved and so were his lectures. He became known to his students as *ons profke* with an unexpressed shade of familiarity and esteem. His activities as a professor were stamped, like the rest of his life, with the sense of his inner life.[41] One should not necessarily conclude that he only taught philosophy because it happened to be the task that his Superiors had thrust upon him. Certainly it is true that his interest in mysticism ran in a different and deeper vein. But he was always conscious of the inter-connection of all branches of science and learning, of the link between matter and spirit, and he felt it his duty to convey this. 'Natural theology' (as a part of philosophy) had, therefore, a special meaning for him, and whether or not a student of philosophy was also to take the course in mysticism, he liked him to have some acquaintance with the concept of God as required by modern man.

The Dutch writer, Godfried Bomans, was among those who attended Brandsma's courses in philosophy and in the history of mysticism. Of the former he remarked that they didn't offer him many new perspectives. The Professor's Frisian distrust of exaggeration, or anything short of accuracy, made him too cautious. But he referred to his classes in the history of mysticism as 'unforgettable hours'. He would always remember him, Bomans said, standing in front of the window that looked out onto a garden of chestnut trees, his fine appearance betraying a quite unique spiritual quality, his soft voice seeking to probe the *clara atque distincta* of Descartes which was so dear to him. The only gesture he permitted himself was that of occasionally raising his hand with thumb and middle finger brought together.[42]

As there was no Carmelite House in Nijmegen, the under-standing was that Titus would spend his Sundays in the friary at Oss. This only involved a short train journey and gave him a change from university life, a chance to relax.

In his rooms at Nijmegen he was quick to show his apprecia-tion for any attention given to him and he never let on to the landlady about his previous ill-health. Eventually, of course, she learned from someone else. His day there began usually at 6 a.m. and was followed by Mass, which he said at the Jesuit Church. He never rested in the afternoons and someone, who was much struck by the details of his daily life, remembered that when he had to go to Rome in 1925, on account of the Holy Year, he continued to type until a few moments before his departure. He then quickly picked up his suitcase, said good-bye and was off.

Father Malachy Lynch, renowned in England for bringing the Carmelites back to Aylesford where once St Simon Stock had resided, recalled that his most vivid memory of Titus was that of him sitting behind his typewriter puffing happily at a cigar. He added that Titus frequently smoked cigars. The greater his concentration, the more he smoked. (Cigars in Holland are as commonplace as cigarettes in England.) Titus once told him that his father always lit up first thing in the morning and offered it up as incense to the Lord. Father Malachy was particularly struck by Titus's industry. 'It was so

quietly done, so naturally, that one might easily have over-
looked it. He was a great example of a priest, fully alive and
with a sense of cheerful urgency.'[43]

It did not take long before all classes of people found their
way to the Spoorstraat where he lived: professors, doctors,
students, the people from Nijmegen, both rich and poor,
Catholics and non-Catholics, among them an old woman whom
he had met on the train and took to his home to make her a
cup of coffee.

At times the housekeeper just left the latch off the lock.
Occasionally she was worried about him and suggested that he
shouldn't receive any more visitors to which Titus replied:
'But it would be sure to be the one who really needed my help.
You'd better let him in.' To encourage the housekeeper he
frequently added: 'We are, after all, in God's hand.'

Regardless of the pressure of work, he was always himself. A
smile would greet everyone that called upon him and he would
listen sympathetically to what they had to say. Among those
visitors there were, as might be expected, many who wasted
his time with trivialities, people whom, not to put too fine a
point upon it, many would consider a nuisance. These, too,
were repeatedly made to feel welcome.

'I have to remind myself that I hold my soul in my own
hands,' he said.

We would like to know whether those hands didn't tremble
at times. They certainly never turned anyone down. And apart
from his Dutch-speaking clientele, he was also (because he
knew Italian) confessor to Italian immigrants, some of whom
also found their way to his home.

During the summer of 1924, Titus went with a few priests
of Frisian origin to Dokkum in Frisia where St Boniface had
been murdered. Boniface, originally called Winifred, was born
in England at the beginning of the 7th century. After entering
a monastery and becoming priest, he went to Frisia to preach
the gospel there. Later Pope Gregory II appointed him to
teach the peoples of Thuringia and Saxony in Germany. With
St Willibrord, another Englishman, who became the first
Archbishop of Utrecht, he returned to the Frisians where he

preached with great success. Soon afterwards he was summoned
to Rome where he was consecrated Bishop, after which he set
out once more for Germany. At length, he went back a third
time to the Frisians. But it was not a case of third time lucky
for the Frisians showed their gratitude by murdering him and
his companions near the river Born. Today his body lies in the
monastery of Fulda in Germany.

Titus and the group of visiting priests decided to form themselves into a committee from which Titus was to emerge as one
of the most influential members. He was bent on the idea of
clubbing together to buy the land where the massacre had
taken place in order to build a national shrine there. To the
admiration of the committee secretary he organized the appeal
and the Press coverage,[44] but not, unhappily, to the admiration
of everyone else. Inevitably, however, startled heads were
raised. The movement caused a certain disquiet, especially in
The Hague, where its motives were viewed with the greatest
possible distrust. Was this not the start of some dangerous
national movement? A protest was made, but Titus succeeded
in soothing the situation down. He did more, he won the day
for the idea of a national shrine.

The first national pilgrimage, led by the Archbishop of
Utrecht and attended by the German bishops of Fulda and
Mainz as well as by two thousand people, took place in August
1926. Titus preached a sermon in Frisian, the first priest to do
so since the Reformation. The event was of momentous
significance for Frisia.

Titus had aimed at forging the links of the religious, cultural,
and historical past with the present. But the Stations of the Cross
had still to be erected in the park and Titus emphasized that
they should be built from the ruins of pre-Reformation monasteries. Later, from his prison during the Second World War,
he was still to remind the committee of the importance of this
and to indicate sites where once monasteries had stood. In his
prison cell he was also to begin work on the meditations for
each Station, but his style lacks his old vigour, even the force
of his earlier prison letters, and a meditation for the last
Station is missing.

After the war his plan was successfully carried out. From all over Frisia stones arrived at Dokkum and for the twelfth Station, which commemorates Christ's death on the Cross, the stones of an ancient monastery near Titus's birthplace were chosen. They didn't think it would detract from the Crucifixion to mention the death of his disciple, Titus Brandsma, in the concentration camp at Dachau.

As we already know, Titus thought the revival and official recognition of the Frisian language a factor of some importance. In this he did not stand alone. He was supported by Protestants, as well. In fact the Frisian version of the *Imitation of Christ* was the result of an ecumenical effort. Titus, already well known in The Hague, took the matter up with the Ministry and succeeded in winning over the Inspector who from that moment onwards gave it his support. According to the Secretary of the Council of Education the passing of the law, which finally accorded recognition to the Frisian language, was mainly due to the efforts of Professor Brandsma.[45]

The thirties saw Titus frequently in Frisia to address, advise, or encourage large and small audiences. But he hardly ever missed his class at the University. Its interest had become very much his own. He stimulated its development and reflected upon its future. The University had not long been in existence when a number of Catholic writers on spirituality decided to publish a periodical about the spirituality of the Low Lands. Under the direction of Dr Brandsma, a team set out to plan and prepare for a definitive history by collating monographs and texts. Along with these, Titus worked out a design for a *Bibliotheca Praereformativa* which, in its turn, was linked to a plan for a *Bibliotheca Neerlandica*. A report of ten years later informs us that from all over Europe about seven collections, the contents of fifty-eight manuscripts, had been photo-copied into folio albums, with a register and systematic index whereby one could check everything. When Titus left there were a hundred and seventy photo-albums.

This achievement aroused great interest in the States whence a delegation was sent to photo-copy the collection at Nijmegen. Titus worked with enthusiasm for the periodical *Ons Geestelyk*

Erf ('Our Spiritual Heritage'), a publication to which experts on mysticism in the Low Lands contributed. It soon became evident that this publication was filling a gap. As to someone's criticism that he was too eclectic, Titus once replied: 'I think he is mistaken about the time I have given to this. Devotion may be bound up with it, but this is essential in a priest. I hope to make as strong efforts in philosophy as I do in mystical science and devotion.'

It cannot be denied that in the realm of philosophy he was making great strides. The University was not merely an employer whom he had to satisfy by filling in a certain number of hours. From the beginning there was no one who journeyed so much on its behalf to make it the concern of all Dutch Catholics.[46]

When he was chosen as chairman of the University Association which concerned itself with scholarships and grants for schools and students, he breathed new life into it. No aspect of University life failed to interest him. The library, the reading-room, the lecture rooms, the professors' quarters, everything concerned him.

He worked so effectively that, on one particular occasion, he convened a special meeting of the Senate in order to discuss whether to buy some large house or to erect a new building in order to bring the scattered parts of the infant University together. Armed with their support he immediately visited Amsterdam and Utrecht, and returned fully supplied with ideas and documents from which he drew up an original plan.

His hopes were not fulfilled. It was only after the destruction caused by the war in 1944 that his plans were remembered. By then he had been dead for two years. But now after the war, the authorities in Nijmegen offered one of the finest open spaces where the new University building eventually arose.

Titus had also worked out the *Corpus Academicum* and the result astounded the professors. His ability and speed of organization were quite remarkable. Someone who once travelled with him on a train was amused to see him sitting back in the compartment drawing up statutes which bore the stamp of considerable insight. It was not the only occasion on which he did his most important work on a train, for he was not a man to waste a moment of the day.

One would have to know the intimate history of the University to evaluate Dr Brandsma's impact on this curious world of professors. It was still young and totally lacking in tradition, but what it lacked in years, it made up in diversity of opinions. Not surprisingly, this led to a certain amount of conflict. It never ceases to amaze those outside the Church that feelings can run as high among men of faith and professed good intentions as among those who are frankly self-interested. But they are, after all, men and their ideas and characters may clash even if they are aiming to establish the common good.

In Nijmegen, the first serious disagreement resulted in the first Rector Magnificus, Dr J. Schrÿnen, becoming almost totally isolated. Undeterred, Titus calmly discussed the issue with his colleagues with the result that the leader of the opposition, a man with a volcanic and dominating temperament, apologized during the next session and shook hands with the Rector Magnificus. As someone testified at the time, Titus was eminently suited to solve the problems of a practical nature, to reconcile conflicting opinions or personal confrontations. In an environment where one clung to one's own opinion because one believed it to be valuable, and to be independently formed after mature thought, he was indispensable as a mediator.[47]

In life, as in his thought, he was always looking out for meeting-points – a man of peace but not a weak-willed or insignificant one. Few had the temerity to abuse him; none doubted his sense of justice. Had he allowed himself to be anyone's puppet he would never have succeeded in gaining the respect of his colleagues, or in becoming the confidant and adviser of men of varying temperaments and characters. Even a particularly troublesome and disagreeable member of the University staff often called on him, pleased to think of himself as Brandsma's friend.

Titus's judgement also carried weight in the Definitory of the Carmelite Province.

Above: The Brandsma family. Titus is shown on the far left

Below: Titus aged seventeen

Brandsma at his ordination

Dr Hubertus Driessen –
Brandsma's master and friend,
later his superior and
collaborator

One day in 1923, Titus was sent on an exploratory mission to Mainz in Germany at the request of the Bishop of Mainz. The bishop had, with the approval of the civil authorities, contacted several Carmelite Provinces asking if they had any interest in a Gothic church in Mainz which, though it had been vacant for over a century, had previously been a Carmelite Church for four centuries. It was in a dreadful state. What should be done about it?

The request had been made during the last few weeks of Titus's stay at Oss. The Provincial had travelled with Titus, although it was not the best moment for travelling in Germany. All hotels had been occupied and, after a long search and considerable difficulty, they were only able to find accommodation in a low-grade inn. Even the door of the room they were given could not be locked. Next morning they visited the Bishop of Mainz, who was very upset that they had not called upon him for hospitality. But the state of the hotel was nothing to that of the church. Here there were no windows and no floor. Notwithstanding, they embarked on a series of conferences about its future, including those with secular authorities such as the French General, Degoutte, who was the commandant of the occupied city, and the German authorities at Darmstadt. Titus travelled from zone to zone and discussed the project, and for each in turn he acted as a willing packhorse, carrying parcels and letters from one to another.

In December 1924 Titus was invited to Mainz to take his place in the procession which walked through the decorated streets of the city and to attend the reopening and consecration of the newly-restored church. The civil authorities showed their pleasure in the restoration with several presents, among them a large tapestry by Caspar de Crayer.

But Titus had not restricted his attention to the Carmelite Church in Mainz. His visits to Germany had given him food for thought in other directions. On Christmas Day, he wrote a detailed report to Dr Hubertus with suggestions for improving the machinery of government in the General Chapter of the Order, referring him to the situation in the German and Austrian Carmelite Provinces. As a postscript he added that, in the past two months, he had been to the Ministry in The Hague eight times in order to get subsidies and that he had been rewarded with several concrete promises.

It was a real joy for Titus when, in the following September, two of the Carmelite students at Oss came to Nijmegen to attend lectures at the University. It was like a dream come true. Years ago, he had begun watching out for potential talent within the Order. It was part of his ambitions for the future of Carmel but he warned his fellow Carmelites, and perhaps himself, when he remarked, 'Let us beware of collective vanity for it is as dangerous as individual pride.'

The student-friars of those early days recalled that Titus' interest in them 'was not something passing, but genuine, personal, and all-embracing. It extended beyond our studies. He often joined us and showed an interest in our hobbies. He didn't just look at the garden which we looked after, but planned it with us. He selected the plants with us with the tact of one who suggests but does not impose.' [48]

During the hours when they didn't have to attend lectures the students were able to go to his rooms. The quiet atmosphere he was used to was thus sometimes interrupted. For student-friars are not essentially different from students the world over. But they appreciated his easy friendship and were impressed by his powers of concentration and ability to be affable and relaxed at the same time as he got on with his work. He worked intensively and rapidly without any sign of being in a hurry. He was a fast typist and while typing out a script he would sometimes join in a conversation, the familiar cigar stuck between his lips. He gave the impression of merely glancing at the papers, but in a conversation about them afterwards he could mention the most minute details. On certain days of the year, some young Carmelites came regularly to Nijmegen for a course. There was then scarcely any room to move, but they were certain of a jovial host who showed interest in all of them.

It was, however, becoming apparent that Titus and his contingency were growing out of their rooms. Now and then Titus took some of them house-hunting with him, conscious of the growing need to expand. But for months nothing better could be found. When he was given a permanent assistant by the name of Denteneer, a move became imperative. It was on the Feast of the Presentation, 1927, that the Provincial finally came to bless the house which Titus had rented in the Kronen-burgersingel. The friars helped to move all his things with the help of a push cart.

It was the end of an era.

Chapter Seven

V.I.P.

∿∿∿∿∿∿∿∿∿∿∿∿∿∿∿∿∿∿∿∿∿∿∿∿∿∿∿

The new house looked out over a park and the ancient Roman fortress of Nijmegen. It was a temporary Carmel of which he was appointed the 'Praeses'. He had, therefore, said good-bye to Oss, where, for the last four years, he had joined the Community on Sundays, and had discussed the affairs of the Order with the Provincial, Cyprianus Verbeek. The latter had gradually become the man through whom Titus kept up his contact with Dr Hubertus. Titus himself referred to this when, now and then, he dropped a line to him. 'I often think of you,' Dr Hubertus would read; but nowhere does the correspondence of the period of 1926–36 reveal anything of Titus's inner life. He was a man to whom reticence was important.

Life at the Kronenburgersingel was as stimulating and as pleasant as a pioneering phase could be. Titus's two adjoining rooms were on the ground floor; bookcases covered the walls, and, by way of a desk, there was a large table on which his card index system stood. Ground plans for a central University building were stuck up on the wall so that he could think and talk them over. He still had to travel but as soon as he returned, he followed the Carmel Rule and saw to it that all his students did the same. He also saw to it that the meals for the student-friars were good and varied for 'students must eat well'. During recreation he was usually the first to offer a light for a pipe or cigar. Though he liked talking about intellectual subjects, he willingly joined in the general conversation and jokes.[49]

Before long it was evident that the foundation at Nijmegen was there to stay and Titus was given the status of Prior. But as the present arrangement was only a temporary one, he was also asked to assume the job of setting up a definitive Priory at Nijmegen.

His opportunity came, perhaps, sooner than he expected. When the Canisius Hospital moved away from the town centre, Titus succeeded in buying the property and transforming it into a monastery with an attractive courtyard. Towards the end of 1929 the Community moved in. The Bishop of Den Bosch was to come for the blessing of the new Carmel on the Feast of the Epiphany on the 6th January, 1930. But Titus didn't want the occasion to remain a domestic one. This Carmel had a special mission. It was to extend the frontiers of the apostolic vocation. He therefore arranged for a symposium which would bring together all searchers of *Ons Geestelyk Erf* ('Our Spiritual Heritage').

It was to become a congress of the intellectual elite of Holland and Vlaanderen in Belgium. Titus himself opened the proceedings with a dissertation on the mysticism of Carmel. It was a happy moment for him when he could show them his first album with its photo-copies of manuscripts, for the album had just been completed. It was the beginning of a new intellectual climate which combined the spiritual and the scholarly in a way which he had always imagined and hoped for.

He would have liked to arrange a similar meeting for the following year. He even drew up a programme. But some of the participants thought he was going a bit too fast and so the idea was put aside. Yet, in a few years, he was to see three more symposia of this kind. They took place in 1932, 1934 and 1936. In 1929, just before the first symposium, he had been to Spain to study the common denominators in Spanish and Dutch mysticism. He visited Madrid, Burgos, Toledo, Seville, Avila, and Montserrat. Whether this expedition actually helped his research it is difficult to say for he never made any definite references to the conclusions he drew from it. His Spanish companion, Simon Besalduch, however, was amused when, on one occasion, they paused for a meal and he leaned forward to pay the bill to find that Titus had got in before him. He protested, but Titus waved him aside with a charming smile:

'El banco de Espana pagara,' he said ('the bank of Spain shall pay').[50]

The one regret that still worried Titus was that circumstances prevented him from devoting more of his time to the publication of the works of St Teresa of Avila. In the Carmel's study centre at Merkelbeek, Dr Hubertus worked steadily on his side of the venture. Titus could not have failed to be aware of this when he called on him. On one such occasion he told him, 'Of course, there are many things in my life that I regret, but none more than that the publication of St Teresa's works still remains unfinished, for which you, partly on my account, do so much work.' [51]

When Father Malachy Lynch visited him at Nijmegen, he was shown an original work by St Teresa, written 'Currente calamo'. Titus's face lit up with admiration as he held it, hardly daring to let it out of his hands.[52] He was so well versed in her writings that he knew *The Interior Castle* practically by heart. He always stressed that 'St Teresa paints the mystical life as something which develops in the soul, according to the latter's natural ability, and as the ultimate realization of man's power. One should read the works to see what a high place reasoning and logical evolution hold in her philosophy. Full of gratitude she says that in one moment of elucidation given by God the soul learns more than by years of study and active contemplation. But she never neglects contemplative prayer, meditation, and active contemplation. She also always appreciates deeply the guidance of a scientific director.' [53]

St Teresa was lofty if not practical. So was her disciple, Titus Brandsma. Over and over again we find him pointing out that, among the mystics, we must learn to distinguish between the characteristics of mysticism essential to them all and the accidental characteristics due to their personal environment. If we do that, he would insist, we would not hesitate to claim that the road to mysticism is also open to modern man, and fundamentally not different from what it has always been.

While the second symposium on mysticism was taking place during Easter Week 1932, Titus was already engaged in preparing the National Marian Congress that was to take place

a few months later. It was to commemorate the fifteenth
centenary of the Council of Ephesus which had declared Mary
to be *Theotokos* ('Bearer of God' or 'Mother of God'), the ancient
title of the Virgin Mary which was originally declared in order
to solve an outstanding dispute concerning the divine and
human nature of her Son.

At the first committee meeting which took place at his
Priory, Titus had tabled several practical points: the historic
foundation of the forthcoming congress; the question of a
statue to be chosen; the processional route; the question of
participation and decorations. Here his pen seemed to poise.
Processions were not popular in severe, serene Holland. But
his mind had gone back to what he had witnessed a few
years earlier in Spain and he wondered if each of the many
churches in Nijmegen might not pull its weight and accept
its own particular responsibility in making it a memorable
occasion.

Why not, in fact, all copy Spain and join in one glorious
celebration and procession? For the moment his feet seemed to
have left the ground. Did he realize, some of his colleagues
asked, that he wasn't living in exuberant Spain but in reserved
Holland? Where did this passion for display come from? Titus
later admitted that he had encountered a great deal of stiff
opposition; it had been quite a struggle for him to get his plans
accepted. But accepted they were. The chairman of the committee was amazed at Titus's strenuous efforts. For three days in
August, representatives of the Government, bishops, professors,
and various delegations came to attend the Centenary cele-
brations.

Nevertheless, successful as the large-scale event turned out to
be, Titus asked himself why other denominations could not have
been persuaded to join in this tribute to the Mother of God.
His thoughts turned especially to the Orthodox Christians in
the East, whose devotion to Mary was so renowned and where
the Council, which was being celebrated, had originally taken
place. But he was also thinking about his own Protestant
countrymen: had they been there, he thought, they would have
seen that our respect for Our Lady does not detract in any way

from our worship of God. In this Titus was ahead of his time. For hardly any contact existed between the churches. By asking such questions openly, he was, however, creating an awareness and showing a personal readiness which was eventually to make its mark.

For the last eight years before the Second World War, Titus directed the annual procession at Nijmegen. The more sophisticated could not understand how he could contemplate such a mass demonstration. But this was to under-estimate the strong impetus which drove him outside the mere intellectual sphere. He looked upon 'the popular' aspect as the lesser of two evils. Besides, he had great respect for the senses. They must sometimes be allowed their due, though he did his best to keep the standard of the occasion on a high level.

He, himself, on Trinity Sunday, could be seen wearing the white Carmelite cloak and walking calmly in the procession. He did so with complete tranquillity, remembering that, centuries ago, Frisia used to walk in procession on the same day and he expressed the hope that the future would see it doing the same.

The year 1932, which had seen the official opening of Nijmegen's Carmel together with the first symposium on mysticism, as well as the National Marian Congress, had still another event in store: Titus Brandsma was chosen as Rector Magnificus of the University of Nijmegen for the academic year 1932–33. On October 17th, he gave his opening address in the hall of the University. His subject was: The Concept of God. It caused a great stir and drew the interest of the nation. In fact, it was considered as something of a theological breakthrough.

'Why,' Titus asked, 'were the intellectuals everywhere in the world turning away from God in such large numbers?'

He referred to the contrary ideologies of the contemporary world, signalling out the conflicting views about God as being the most serious. Could modern man form his own image about God? Titus was sure he could. Had not every age done so? Here he reached the main part of his argument: a penetrating investigation into the historic concepts of God. After analyzing

and synthesizing these, he posed the questions anew: 'What is
our concept of God? Is it strong enough to hold modern man?'
Superficially, he agreed, it did not seem to be.

Titus conceded that it was not possible to give an easy answer
to the question as to which was the concept of God that carried
the most conviction, that is, the one best suited to contemporary
needs. The reason, he explained, is that there is so little unity
underlying modern thought that one would be obliged to
consider an endless series of successive images to arrive at even
an approximate answer. Yet he believed that there are three
tendencies that point the way to modern man's concept of God.

First, he thought, there is the tendency towards a better
metaphysical insight. As a result of the currents of materialism,
especially under the influence of evolutionary thinking, the
mind has begun to look for a unity that satisfies the mind and
that lies beyond the appearances. Another tendency in modern
thought is the intuitive character ascribed to human knowledge.
We are offered a great variety of opinion about this intuitive
nature of knowledge, ranging from Max Scheler to Bergson.
Titus remarked that he merely wished to draw our attention
to the value which we now attach to it. At times man is brought
to accept values which the mind cannot strictly prove but which
man nevertheless grasps as revealed in, and through, nature
itself. The third characteristic, closely linked to the latter, Titus
called the pragmatic tendency. 'At this stage man has accepted
a truth and acts upon it. Man is, after all, not merely a being
that knows his whole nature leads him to the truth and keeps
him related to it. By his deeds, man is simultaneously partly
consciously and partly unconsciously led to the discovery and
revelation of the truth. Here, too, we see strong nuances. On
the whole, however, man is becoming less shut up in himself and
is reaching out to the cosmos to which he knows himself
intimately bound. The social and communal aspects are, in
fact, being consciously grasped within himself. Those who view
history philosophically do not despair and, happily, those who
reason dispassionately also expect that the crisis shall be overcome. But what is the basis for this confidence? It is first of all
based on the nature of man, for nature calls forth from man a

healthy reaction which leads him to counteract evil. Nature is prior to doctrine. And behind nature there is God, the God who created nature and preserves it and who operates in, through, and with it, and whose work and whose being can be recognized therein by man's powers of reason.'

For this reason Titus suggests that: 'We must first of all see God as the very source of our being, hidden in the innermost part of our nature and yet visible, a God who, after an initial effort of abstraction by the mind, becomes clearly recognizable. Then, when one has acquired this habitual disposition, we will see Him by intuition without any repeated intellectual effort, so that we see ourselves in continuous contemplation of Him and adore Him not only in our own being but also in nature and in the Universe.'

Titus then pointed out that this natural concept of God, accommodated to the philosophical current of our time, becomes more distinct in proportion as we, in our turn, bring these characteristics of our knowledge of God as revealed in revelation, to the forefront of our mind.

'Where faith, hope, and charity are being exercised in a most heroic manner, there we experience the nearness of the divine. There God confronts us as it were, through the person who exercises these virtues and anyone who witnesses it will fall under the spell of the divine radiance.

'It is not enough that we perform good deeds, but the good deeds themselves must spring forth from a conscious union with God. That consciousness must become the strong incentive for the deed. Nor is faith in God sufficient; it is to be seen as alive in our actions and thus will it reveal its value.'

Titus felt convinced that such a concept of God would not only appeal strongly to the modern world but, once firmly rooted, it would be capable of withstanding many an onslaught. He thought that it would help man to break out of his feeling of isolation as he would thus know himself united with all men in, through, and with God. Referring to what history has taught us, Titus felt obliged to voice a twofold warning. Human reasoning must always remain the basis of human under-standing. The contemplation of God will then eventually be-

come second nature to us and appear to our consciousness as
an intuition. We must never lose sight of the road that led us
to contemplation for if we did, our contemplation would lose
its force and our deeds would lose their impact just as a
pragmatic interpretation would lead to exterior behaviourism.
The history of our spiritual life has clearly illustrated how a
one-sided view of the exercise of virtues can lead to exterior
behaviourism.

Alluding to the fact that we welcome images or examples,
Titus concluded his one-hour speech with these simple words:
'For the development of our concept of God we do not lack an
image or an example. For there is the Virgin who became the
mother of the incarnate God, who gave God to us as Emmanuel,
who died on the cross so that we might live in union with God
and be filled with His grace. In the realm of grace, He was
thus born in us. It was to perfect the union with God in the
order of nature (to make that union still more intimate and
abundant) that the Mother of God offered herself as a model
for this most intimate union. May we always have that model
before our eyes. She is, in fact, more than a model. Mary has
been called to direct our vision towards God.

'Just as we, led by Revelation, acknowledge the child in her
arms as God, thus may she guide our minds to the contemplation of God in all the things He has created. As He lived in her,
He may live in us, and born of our deeds, make His entry into
the world.'

His carefully developed theme emphasized, as the mystics
have always taught, that the road to God is the road within
oneself: 'We must see God first of all in the innermost part of
our being . . . and this must reveal itself in our words and deeds,
radiate our entire being and conduct.'

Titus wished to show his contemporaries that they, too, could
discover God within themselves, and he reminded them that
everyone is called to mysticism.

Discussions about his address went on for a long time. A
theologian of the Protestant Faculty of Theology requested his
students to study the entire text. By now the name of Dr
Brandsma was known throughout the country.

Ironically, it was the same year that Hitler rose to power in
Germany. It was also the year that the concentration camp of
Dachau, where Titus was to die, was opened.

During that same academic year, many towns in Holland
were to see Titus and hear him speak about union with God,
for it was the fifth centenary of the death of St Liduina of
Schiedam, a town near Rotterdam.

As a young girl, Liduina had fallen on the ice and never
recovered from the injuries she received. For thirty-eight years
she was bedridden and suffered terribly. She did not complain.
Instead she offered herself to God and became a great mystic.
She died in her native town, Schiedam, in 1433. Her case
fascinated Titus and his interest in her touched off a response
in his fellow countrymen. He was even invited to speak about
her over Radio Hilversum. It is curious that the same year that
saw him become Rector Magnificus of the University of
Nijmegen should see him, evening after evening, speaking in
every part of Holland about a girl who had found union with
God through suffering.

The rise of National Socialism in Germany was not without
its repercussions in Nijmegen University. Some of the noisier
students paraded through the town, bearing the red flag. The
Rector, however, did not appear too disturbed. In spite of
protests from other students he did not publicly chastise them.
Once again he repeated that one should treat people as if they
were what they ought to be. It expressed one of his deepest
convictions.

He did, of course, refer to the incident, though without
making an issue of it. In days when the trend towards radicalism
was running high, such things, he reminded them, were quite
to be expected as there are always those who are easily carried
away. But he expressed his confidence that the students as a
whole were seeking for true values and more stable concepts.
In moments of conflict or tension, Titus was always careful to
try first of all what could be achieved by mediation and it was
because of his serene approach that he made himself acceptable
to so many elements.

The same qualities distinguished his articles in the Press

which were often addressed to those who feared the rise of an intellectual proletariat. The polemics that followed them indicate that this was felt to be an issue of some importance at the time. In his address at the University, Titus said that he could not see this as a danger; that by extending the possibilities of higher education, spiritual values were being made available to a greater part of humanity. Surely, this could not be wrong.

But even he, who had on several occasions to seek employment for intellectuals, agreed in his answers to questions that he foresaw a temporary crisis. But one should not exaggerate it. The great thing was to keep calm. Successive events have in fact proved him right.

His was a familiar face on the ferry that so frequently crossed the river Waal. As one critic sarcastically remarked to him. 'I thought that Carmelites were self-effacing people, but one meets this friar everywhere. One cannot cross the Waal in a boat without you being there to the fore in your white cloak.'

Titus did not appear upset but replied with equanimity that he valued the wearing of the white cloak as it signified the protection of the Mother of God.

On the evening that the University celebrated its tenth anniversary, the students and alumni went to the local hotel where the Senate of the University was holding a celebration. Later that same evening a group of them went, with torches alight, to the Carmel and called out for Titus. A tumultuous ovation broke out when he appeared, trying in vain to quieten them.[54] It was a touching tribute from the University he loved, for the previous evening Titus had ended his term as Rector Magnificus. In a report of thirty-nine pages he had summed up the existing state of the University. The figures showed how worthwhile it had all been. It was a great joy for him when, shortly afterwards, he succeeded in taking over the Church of St Augustine for the University and saw it placed under the care of Carmel.

Later, the Archbishop of Utrecht donated to this church the relics of St Radbout who had himself been Archbishop of Utrecht and after whom the governing institute of the University had been named. But the Archbishop was careful to get

Titus to look into the authenticity of the relics first. Titus set to his task with his customary zeal and soon satisfied him on this score, summing up his findings in a detailed report.

During his researches into the field of mysticism, Titus had by now travelled to France, Italy, Spain, and Germany. In 1935 he was asked by the General of the Order to address the Carmelite houses of New York, Chicago, Washington, Niagara Falls, Middletown, and Allentown. Today, it is quite usual for a professor to cross the Atlantic, but in the thirties it was still something of an event.

On his way to America, Titus stayed at the Carmelite Priory at Kinsale in Ireland to brush up his English. He had learnt some English at school but as he had never been to an English-speaking country, his knowledge of the language was very limited.

Father Malachy Lynch, who was to effect the return of the Carmelites to Aylesford in England, was, at the time, Master of Novices at Kinsale. He had met Titus at Nijmegen not long before, for when he was in Rome attending a conference of all Masters of Novices of the Order, the General had suggested that those who could, should pay a visit to the Dutch Province and perhaps glean some inspiration from doing so. Hearing the name of Titus Brandsma mentioned several times, Father Malachy decided to return to Ireland via Holland. There he stayed for several days and helped Titus to put his American lectures into English.

It was on that occasion that Titus promised Father Malachy that he, in turn, would stop at Ireland on his way to America and come for a few days to Kinsale.

Once he had arrived, Titus's main desire was to meet and get to know the fishermen. What impressed Father Malachy in particular was that immediately after his arrival at Kinsale, his first visit, after seeing the Prior, was to the sick of the House. Father Malachy's impression was that Titus was the happiest person he had ever known, one who had the faculty of spreading happiness all round him.

Although he was such a distinguished scholar, Titus never sought to impress or overpower any one. Titus himself appreciated the good things of life as he often used to remark. He had never drunk Irish whiskey before, but he was delighted with the discovery. He drank several Irish whiskies but to Father Malachy's intense relief it did not seem to have the slightest effect upon him.[55]

Titus was certainly not a Jansenist. Nor was he the sort of man who would look for discomfort or pain unnecessarily; he was merely careful, when it came his way, not to let it weigh him down. While he was actually on the Atlantic, Titus received a distress signal from the Dutch *Catholic Encyclopaedia*. They urgently awaited his scholarly contribution on mysticism. When would it be ready? As he had taken the initiative in this enterprise (he had planned it and spent many years rigorously censoring every line of its twenty-five parts), he felt obliged to get down to it at once.

When he reached America, he observed that it was by no means closed to mysticism. Standing before the microphone he said: 'Everything which exists, exists through God's hand. . . . As He is always so present to us . . . we must learn how to live with Him. We must learn from our fathers about the interior life which united them with Him.'

In Chicago they asked for his manuscript and published his series of talks under the title *Carmelite Mysticism* which, in the main, followed the contents of his magnificent contribution to the *Dictionnaire de Spiritualité*. No less an authority than Debognie hailed it as outstanding.

When he visited Ontario he went on to say: 'I am there contemplating the imposing Niagara Falls; from their high channel I can see them rushing down ceaselessly . . . I say to myself: What is surprising is the marvellous and complex possibility of the waters; if they were not drawn down by the great mass of the earth, if they were not fluid, if they did not have the capacity for absorbing the light down to their smallest drops, would we have this avalanche of crystal before our wonder-struck eyes, and this rainbow at our feet? . . . There are probably thousands of men and women who come here and are merely alarmed by the tumult of the waters, by their rising clouds and their brilliant flight into the distance. The savage music seizes hold of their whole being, the play of the colours dazzles them when the sun dives in, when the reflection of the rock and the silver emerald-green pass through alternately. With some their contemplation is more reasoned, with others it is more sensitive; if the two interior movements become merged in each other, since the object and the subject wish to be united, the enjoyment will then be more uplifted. The more the possibilities of contemplation are brought together, the higher will be the quality of the joy. Sight and sound may be enchanted but [so] also the reason, which thinks over everything which God has placed in these fugitive elements . . . And I see God in the work of His hands and the marks of His love in every visible thing . . . and it sometimes happens that I am seized by a supreme joy which is above all other joys.' [56]

Titus also received an invitation to address the University of Washington. In his address he pointed out that, with the branching out of Carmel into various European countries in the 13th century, St Simon Stock had found it necessary to adapt the existing Rule while maintaining it spiritually in the tradition of Carmel. When St Teresa of Avila set about restoring Carmel she used this adapted Rule and she, too, had admitted that it was sometimes difficult to decide where to draw the line in regard to active apostolate. Titus commented: 'That in itself is a great tribute to the spiritual genius of St Simon.'[57]

He also referred to that remarkable man, Jean du Moulin, who had pointed out that it was important for the young members of the Order to be set firmly on the road to contemplation so that, when grown up and confirmed in this, they could never really lose the habit of contemplation. Emphatically, and not for the first time, he rejected the idea that the mystical life is not for everyone. 'Of course,' Titus added, 'it is and ever remains a gift of God, but God has made our nature susceptible to it.'

Once again Titus was requested to leave his script behind. It was published in the form of nine lectures under the title *The Beauty of Carmel*. To read these almost thirty-five years later, one is struck by how fresh and readable they are today.

His strenuous tour over, Titus returned to Nijmegen. Shortly before he had left for America, the Archbishop of Utrecht had requested him to become the National Spiritual Adviser to the Catholic journalists. He was already well-known to many editors for his contributions. In accepting this new challenge, although he did not know it at the time, he was to take the path which was to lead him straight to his death seven years later.

The Hierarchy knew that they had chosen a man who would not take his new duties lightly. When Titus went to America he was careful, wherever he was on tour, to seek information about the American Press, bearing in mind the new office that awaited him at home in Holland. One of his first contacts in America was with someone who taught journalism at the University of Washington, so that on his return, when he first met the Dutch editorial boards and journalists, they were taken aback by his detailed technical knowledge.

As in other circles he had frequented, he was soon warmly welcomed and sadly missed when he was prevented from attending editorial meetings. They quickly learnt that he didn't see his function as a censor but as an adviser and a constructive one at that. The chairman of these meetings remarked: 'It was quite apparent from his manner, from his advice, from his attitude towards the opinions of others, from his readiness to give himself, that this man wasn't thinking of himself but only wished to serve the cause to which he clearly had given his heart and energy. . . . It was always a disappointment when he could not attend. One was really glad to see him present at our meetings.'[58]

He was soon to come forward with a proposal that was only to come into operation after the war. In 1948, a special training centre for journalists, which he had proposed ten years earlier, was opened at Nijmegen. Four and a half years after his appointment the chairman asked whether there was one important town left in Holland where Dr Brandsma had not been in the interests of journalism.[59]

It was obvious that his dynamic personality and personal philosophy were geared to the solution of modern man's problems. He had scant sympathy with empty speculations. Everything had to be tried and proved although he had a great quality of dash. But his proverbial enthusiasm sometimes drove him to lengths which were considered un-Dutch, if not excessive. He hated to see any avenue left unexplored. On one occasion this received a literal interpretation. The Priory in Nijmegen was separated from the parish church by several houses and a road. Titus suggested digging a tunnel to solve the problem. Needless to say this particular suggestion was brushed aside. Again at Merkelbeek, where the Carmel's House of Studies needed a larger garden, he suggested a viaduct across to a nearby and available piece of land. One could see that he took the financial aspects rather lightly or, perhaps, he felt that creativity was a rare gift, and that it was up to him to make suggestions while leaving it to others to decide when and whether they were practical. In this he was not unlike Winston Churchill.

More than once he alluded to this characteristic to his students. 'Christ cannot live in us,' he once remarked, 'if we don't allow Him a chance . . . we are cowardly and timid. . . . Our motto is not to exaggerate, and we are so careful to live up to it that we suppress all spontaneity. We don't call it that of course. We say we are being prudent. . . . We prefer to keep our heads cool. We are so concerned about public opinion that there is too much emphasis on reserve' (and he might have added: too much fear of making mistakes), 'that one looks in vain for charity, sacrifice and courage.' [60]

He once called himself a 'Child of his own time' and certainly the young seem to have considered him one of themselves.

When he was imprisoned by the Nazis, Titus was ordered to put into writing what his people thought, felt, and believed. No one could have borne better witness than this Carmelite priest.

No wonder, then, that journalists found in him an ideal adviser. He become their confidant in private matters as well, took steps to reconcile conflicting parties and even attempted to arrange a retreat for them.

He once succeeded in bringing eight of them together for a day of retreat and recollection. It was in 1937, when they met just outside Nijmegen. Here, he spoke to them about 'God's place in the Press and on the desk', and 'gentleness and humility in journalism, with its limits and demands'. He dealt with these topics in an up-to-date style, allowing ample opportunity for exchange of opinions. The small group who attended were deeply impressed.

As it was still the age of specialization, there were not many who saw that it was possible to be a professor, research worker, and journalist as well as a priest and monk. It puzzled some, much though they admired him. Titus once told a caller that his lecture on some point of history had been criticized by a newspaper and called 'more of a conference to non-Catholics'. To the surprise of the visitor, Titus didn't feel in the least hurt. His eyes were lit up. Some people voiced their regret that Brandsma didn't stick to philosophy. He was well aware of this, but he was not the man to evaluate knowledge as an end in itself; for him it was a means and those who had nominated him to the University must have known it too.

Yet one might well ask whether it was a defect in him that the social and priestly sides of his character were both so strongly developed that his ability for scientific work could not hope to manifest itself to its full potential. The University had some reason to be jealous. It was young and still had to make a name for itself. It laid emphasis on scientific publications, and Titus did not always meet the very high demands they wanted from their first team of professors. But, in fact, in spite of his dedication to various other causes and the time he gave to individuals and their personal troubles, he still accomplished some very important things as a University professor. He certainly raised himself above the level of mediocrity and was acknowledged to be a very learned man. The professors, Van Ginneken and Mulder, are on record as having said that no matter how scrupulous they were in their scientific research, Dr Brandsma could point to neglected aspects or indicate other sources. It is also beyond question that he regarded his professorship as his chief duty. He was much preoccupied with the status and sphere of the University. Much of what Titus did and stood for actually contributed to its growing reputation. His commissioned history of mysticism not only gave him personal satisfaction but a chance to provide Nijmegen with a Christian tradition.

He was soon to see his hopes and expectations materialize and his position at the University certainly gave him a platform which strengthened his influence in big and small matters, in public and private affairs. It enabled him to use his talents to the maximum effect.

Let us return to the Priory at the Doddendaal. The main inspiration of his life was that of Carmel. His life as a novice, and his references during lectures and as a sixty-year-old prisoner to the lessons of St Teresa are very revealing. All his life he seemed to have drawn strength from them. He had plenty of excuse to be dispensed from the Rule but he would never consider this alternative. Quite possibly he felt that this is where he had to draw the line.

At half past five in the morning he would be in choir for meditation. Only a direct order from his Superior could stop him. When, during the winter of 1939, he was just recovering from an infection, it was he who requested to be allowed in early chapel again. As he was still under doctor's orders the Superior referred him to his doctor who refused permission for at least another month. Hardly was the month over when Titus renewed his request, which was then granted. His Superior abided by the doctor's verdict but he couldn't help noticing with what difficulty Titus got up after the prayer to the Holy Spirit. Titus was determined to live the Carmelite life as fully as possible. The Divine Office appeared to have on him the effect of a tonic. His confrères remarked that his duties and concerns didn't seem to cause him any distraction; he left them all behind when he went into chapel. He was so absorbed by the significance of the Divine Office that, from time to time, he had been 'carried away' and they had to point out to him that his voice in choir was too loud. Occasionally it happened that the Community recitation of the Office coincided with a Mass Titus had to celebrate in order that other priests of the Community could be fitted into a time schedule. Though Titus never sought an exception for himself, here he tried to change the time of his Mass with someone else so that he would not

have to miss part of the Office. At one time there was a discussion about exempting the student-friars who went to the
University.

'If that is going to be tabled in the Definitory,' he said, 'I
shall speak out against it with all available energy. If there is
anyone who has grounds for exemption it is me, and I won't
dream of it.'[61]

Possibly he recalled the warning of Carmel's reformer, John
Soreth, against privileges for academics.

For several years, Titus was Prior of his own foundation. As
Prior he regularly held a Chapter meeting at which he spoke in
a concrete and realistic way. If the friars could work better in
more adequately heated rooms, then they must have them; that
was no luxury, neither were the extra reviews or periodicals if
these were a help to their studies. Moreover, visitors were to be
made welcome and should be offered such things as a cup of tea
or a cigar. Niggardly saving never did anyone any good.
Although he was a gentle man he was fairly strict in regard to
the observance of the Carmel Rule. He was careful to see that
life at Carmel did not degenerate into a routine, as this would
be a formidable obstruction to union with God. One should
fight against allowing oneself to become a 'minimum sufferer',
as he termed it, and he was capable of going into a penetrating
and acute personal diagnosis which sometimes made those
before him feel uncomfortable, even critical.

But his magnanimity and humour soon restored the *status
quo*. In a word, all mediocrity was strange to him. He believed
that it would put up a barrier to a close union with God. His
colleague of many years, the future Provincial, Dr B. Meyer,
remarked that Titus always created the right atmosphere.
During the hectic weeks of examinations he helped out in
several classes but he always tried to come home to meet his
confrères at the longer recreation periods of Tuesday and
Thursday. One evening, one of the priests whose birthday it was
had been assisting in a neighbouring parish and got back late
to hear someone push a piece of paper under the door of his
room; it contained a greeting and good wishes from Titus.

This kind of thing, his colleagues say, was typical of him.

When Dr Hubertus was to celebrate his jubilee, Titus informed
him that he was unfortunately preoccupied the evening before
so that he would not be able to arrive in time for the jubilee
Mass next day. But he got there. He managed to get a lift from
a van driver who left Nijmegen in the early hours of the
morning. He loved to surprise people.

At the beginning of the war, the Procurator visited the
Houses of the Province to rearrange their administration. This
plan did not go down with Titus. When the Procurator came to
see him in order to clarify things, he dismissed his arguments
cursorily. When the Procurator, realizing he could not hope to
convince Titus, referred to his commission and the lengthy
study he had had to make of the subject, Titus suddenly dropped
all his arguments and gave in. They parted with great cordiality.
At the time Titus was no longer Prior although, it will be
remembered, he was to remain an influential voice in the
Definitory.

In 1936, Titus had stepped down as Prior. The advisers to the
Provincial had for some time felt concerned about his financial
management. Titus was made to understand that a 'more
cautious' Prior was required. He made no demur. To all outward appearances he was pleased to be relieved of authority.
He had frequently said: 'Just as we must lose our lives in order
to save them, in the Order it is necessary to lose one's indepen-
dence so that one may gain one which has far wider scope.'

The new Prior was a young man who had much occasion for
being impressed by the humility and obedience of his pre-
decessor. He wondered whether anyone had ever really sounded
the depth of his spiritual life, for Titus was not the type of man
to keep diaries or make notes about his spiritual experiences.
Even his letters are to the point and don't reveal his inner self.
He believed in being reticent.

In his correspondence with Dr Hubertus, though that is
full of the affairs of the Order, the same reticence holds good.
Titus does not refer to his spiritual life. Yet Dr Hubertus, too,
was a great Carmelite.

There is a letter from another Carmelite of stature, Fr
Brenninger, to Hubertus in which he recalls, with some

nostalgia, their daily walks in Rome and their conversations about mysticism and God. In his later years at Merkelbeek, Dr Hubertus continued his hour of meditation every morning on thoughts drawn from the *pars prima* of St Thomas Aquinas; and his ordered life and spirit of prayer were characteristics of the man. This was the man who once told the Provincial that he had come to revere Titus so highly that when, at the beginning of the war in a town in the south of Holland, the rumour spread that St Thérèse of Lisieux had appeared to Father Brandsma and had told him that the war would soon end, Dr Hubertus's reaction was that it didn't surprise him in the least, for he had expected that such a thing might happen to Brandsma any day. When someone telephoned Nijmegen and Titus came to hear all about it, he burst out laughing. The incident shows something of Hubertus's evaluation of Titus as well as of Titus's forthright outlook.

Yet, on one occasion, Titus said to his audience: 'God who lives in us and in whom we live, move and have our being, does not always hide . . . sometimes He replaces the image by the reality, the imagination by the conscious experience. In Holland, too, He has done so.'

Whether the Lord had done this for Titus remains an open question. But all those who observed him, among them many who noticed his defects, remark that when in prayer he gave one the impression of being perfectly calm and absorbed in God. Although he enjoyed travelling, and he had a season ticket on the trains, several who knew him well assure us that he preferred to be at Carmel.[62]

He mixed with great facility in all kinds of circles but was always completely himself; his words and gestures betrayed no trace of artificiality, no concession to a change of audiences. Perhaps his background on the wide open spaces of the Frisian farm may have given him a certain natural disposition that made him a stranger to the nervous tendencies of a great many town-dwellers. The simplicity and spirituality of Carmel would have perfected it. He knew well the words of the Spanish Teresa: *Nada te turbe, nada te espante* . . . ('Let nothing disturb thee; let nothing affright thee. All passeth away. God alone abideth. Patience obtaineth all things. He who hath God can want for nothing. God alone sufficeth'). He was to give a place to these words in his prison cell.

On various public occasions in the thirties he reminded men that the world is in dire need of Christian love. Frequently, he helped people without anyone knowing at the time, accounts of which have only come to light since his death. Once he went to the rescue of a girl who had nearly ruined her life. On another occasion it was the parents of a mentally ill student who appealed to him in time for Titus was able to persuade the boy to become a voluntary patient. He even made his way into prison to talk to people who had forgotten themselves. Sometimes, even Religious Communities other than his own called on him to come to the rescue of one of their members. One evening he telephoned the Mother Superior of a convent and asked her if he could come and see her. Having been assured that he would be welcome, Titus set out through the dark and wet streets of Nijmegen, crossed the river by ferry and after three quarters of an hour reached his destination. To her astonishment, the Mother Superior learnt that his sole objective was to seek some kind of job for an unemployed man. Why hadn't Titus dealt with it over the telephone, or scribbled a little note, or told the man to try for himself at the convent? The answer is simple. Titus had made that man's anxiety his own and so did all he could to ensure a living for him, though it cost him an evening of valuable time.

Until his arrest, Titus went every Sunday morning to an old people's home. He had heard that they were looking for a priest to say Mass there but that they could not afford to give him the customary stipend. Titus persuaded his Superior to allow him to take on the job. He always gave a short simple sermon and included a few words for the Sisters who ran the home. The Sister in charge of the sacristy tended to see things in a rather sombre light. He freed her from her depression without using many words. 'It was as if he pushed you,' she remarked later, 'and you could live on it for a long time.'

He once told her: 'We must not wish to see everything but live by faith; that is a darkness, a dark tunnel; you must pass through it, Sister.' He then suggested a few lines from St John of the Cross.

Sometimes people could not remember exactly what he had told them, but the spiritual malaise had lifted. 'Our love must be proverbial. No one is to surpass us in love,' Titus had preached; in practice he tried to live up to it. Hundreds have met him there at the Doddendaal, always calm, greeting everyone with a smile and outstretched hands. However trivial the matter, he proved to be a sympathetic listener, so that it sometimes happened that, even at 11.30 a.m. he still had not breakfasted because people had been calling upon him nonstop. The sad reality of the division among Christians was another cause that could not escape his attention and concern.

When, in the years after the First World War, the journeys of the Primate of Lemberg, Count Andreas Sceptycki, drew the attention of the West to the fate of the Christians in the East, Titus asked to be allowed to join the Apostolate for Reunion. His own missionary aspirations were to remain unfulfilled; that became clear with his appointment to the University. But hardly anyone had joined the movement for Reunion when he came forward, and, before long, directed a study-group among the students at the University. At first he hesitated to take the chair but, eventually, he did so and kept this position till the very end.

Even members from abroad were advised to go and see Professor Brandsma. In the Reunion movement he became an enthusiastic supporter and wise friend.[63] This also brought him into contact with the future Bishops of Haarlem and Rotterdam.[64] The 'minutes' of the meetings show us how ably he spoke his mind about all its affairs. But once again his particular gifts were called for when there was a vehement clash of opinion. The issue around which the crisis evolved this time was over which should take precedence: a study-and-action group which was to aim at making the Dutch aware of the fate of the Christians in the East, or an all-out effort actually to help those in the East.

Messages and circular letters went to and fro. Titus wanted to prevent the opponents of both sides from becoming too entrenched. His efforts to bring them together were endless. At the end of a heated session his proposal, which asked for both groups to sacrifice something of their demands, was at last accepted. It was agreed that the study group was to continue with its main purpose of giving direct help to the Christians in the East.

In his own heart Titus cherished the hope of seeing a kind of Oriental Institute within the framework of the University, that in due course might be expanded to include a course for those who aspired to work as priests in the East. In 1937, after many serious discussions, the Apostolate for Reunion agreed to support and help finance a faculty for Eastern theology and missionary work.

It was typical of Titus that he stepped down as chairman of the University study-group at once and offered it to the newly-appointed leader of the new faculty. But his desire for unity made him raise the issue on their behalf in all parts of the country as well as in many of his articles. It was, on the whole, a happy, energetic phase of his life, full of opportunities realized and of hopes fulfilled, which was drawing to a close. But if he had gained much, he had also given much.

It was not enough. Of such a man events sometimes demand all he has, his life. This, though he did not know it, was the prospect before him.

PART THREE

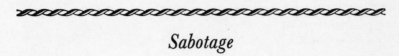

Sabotage

Chapter Eight

A MATTER OF CONSCIENCE

Certainly there was nothing in the early months of 1940 to suggest Titus's imminent death. He was in excellent spirits in spite of the fact that his physical health was not all that good. It had never fully recovered after the worrying period that had undermined it in 1939. Photographs of these years show him comparatively sturdy and, if not actually good-looking, pleasant, and serene in countenance.

Perhaps it was his camera face. For at moments of crisis or uncertainty it was amazing how insignificant he could sometimes look. When, as Rector Magnificus of the University, he travelled to Rome and called on Cardinal Bisleti the situation became almost comic. The Cardinal, as hard of hearing as he was immense in girth (in an age when, among prelates and opera singers, size was an almost immediate indication of rank), did not suspect that he was face to face with the Rector of the University. 'Ah,' he said, bustling slowly forward, 'couldn't the Rector Magnificus himself come? Is he ill?'

Titus introduced himself again.

'Ah, that is a pity,' murmured the Cardinal sympathetically.

Realizing, at last, the nature of the misunderstanding, Titus raised his voice and repeated who he was.

The Cardinal looked at him with astonishment: '. . . é lei, é lei . . . ? Are you he?'

At times it seemed as if Titus were deliberately acting the comedian, that he actively enjoyed underplaying his hand. More than once, he was taken for a brother when he went to answer the door himself, still wearing the apron left over from some household task.

In the course of 1937, the temporary lull in his ill-health was intercepted by some disquieting symptoms. One day he told his Prior: 'I am afraid there is something wrong. I can't keep standing up anymore. My knees are failing me.'

The symptoms suggested some form of paralysis. Suddenly he ran a high temperature and had to be nursed all night. During the last years one of his sisters had developed a complaint of the spinal marrow which led in the end to complications of the brain. Titus let on that he thought he might be heading in the same direction.

The doctors thought it advisable to examine him. An infection of the spinal marrow, with a deviation in the central nervous system, did, in fact, come to light. But with the help of medical attention he learnt to cope with the uncomfortable symptoms, though, during the autumn of 1939, people noticed that all was not well with him. He looked exhausted; he had spells of giddiness and his memory began to fail him occasionally. It probably accounted for some severe criticisms passed on his vagueness and forgetfulness by his students at this time. Yet, even during this period, he continued to charm some of them with the spontaneity and freshness with which he drew on examples from ordinary life and from their own lives too. No detail was too trivial, no observation too slight with which to stimulate and hold their interest.

In December a serious infection of the urine tract added to his trials but the patient remarked with assurance that the discovered coli-bacilli had nothing whatsoever to do with the enormous pressure of work. He expressed the diagnosis in the style of an international news agency. 'The bacilli,' he remarked quite gayly, 'are very modern and treacherous. They begin an offensive without a declaration of war.'[65]

It was four months before Hitler's armies invaded Holland – like the bacilli, without a declaration of war.

Things continued to go up and down for Titus. The bacilli came and went, returned and disappeared again. On Christmas Day he said Mass in the Priory chapel. On other days he appeared dazed and half doped by the medicines he was taking. Then suddenly, he started to improve rapidly. To the surprise of everyone in Nijmegen he went to the Rector Magnificus'

New Year reception though it was a bitterly cold day. 'Things are not bad with me,' he wrote, 'though I am not yet a hundred per cent.'

He decided to cancel a few lectures and conferences. 'I am getting so many admonitions to cut down on my work, that I cannot ignore them altogether.'

Perhaps he passed a few pleasant hours with reading the *Album Amicorum* with which he had been presented the previous October when he had celebrated the fortieth anniversary of his profession in the Carmel Order. There is something moving about this collection in which so many pay tribute to a much-loved man. There are pages in Italian, German, Latin, French, and Greek. The great figures in the Carmel Order were represented: General Doswald, his Spanish and Italian confrères, and Malachy Lynch who enlarged, with humour, upon Titus' perennial 'gift of youth'. The Greeks recalled his efforts for Christian unity. The pages carry the signatures of many Bishops and University authorities, of students, secular priests, and representatives of various associations, and, not to be forgotten, inhabitants of his native Friesland.

Titus lengthened his stay at the Priory in Merkelbeek where it was his habit to go for a break after Christmas. The winter was severe. He stayed indoors more, occupying himself with studying and writing after Mass in the well-heated monastic church.

Meanwhile, tension was mounting in western Europe. The threat of war had become very real. In April, Titus went to Amsterdam for a thorough medical examination. He was suffering from headaches and periods of failure of memory. The source of infection could not be reached, but his stomach which had been the victim of so many medicines must be given a rest from them. Doctors tried rinsing the bladder, a painful ordeal which, however, was worth it for it gradually restored his constitution and neutralized the poisonous activity of the bacilli.

On the 10th May, 1940, Hitler's armies invaded Holland. At 4 a.m. the country awoke to the sound of sirens and aeroplanes.

Titus started to say Mass; then he got down to his work, occasionally interrupting it to listen to the news on the wireless.

At about nine o'clock he set out for the University as examinations had been scheduled for that day.

The streets were crowded with people, especially on and around the church steps. The sound of distant shooting could be heard all over the town. At the University, the examiners didn't keep their candidates long. The questions were as vague as the answers.

At the priory they spent the evening in the cellar. Someone had brought an old, blind priest who sat in the midst of a rather nervous group while Titus did his best to make it as pleasant as possible for him. When, later in the evening, the sound of gun-fire became less, he retired to his own room. Within a few days, Holland was forced to capitulate.

Towards the end of May, Titus called upon Mgr Paolo Giobbe, the Papal Internuntius in The Hague. His former pupil, the Armenian Patriarch Agagianian, had suggested his name as someone who might help in regard to the Christians in the East.[66] The Internuntius and Titus discussed the situation which had now become extremely grave, as all connections with the East were cut. Patience seemed the only answer, and it was the one Titus advised in his letter to the Armenian Patriarch.

Several professors from Nijmegen University were imprisoned by the new regime. One of them was allowed to receive a letter from Titus, who quoted the words of St Teresa of Avila: 'Let nothing disturb you. . . . Patience overcomes everything. . . .'

Hitler's forces began their deliberate attempts to curtail the freedom of the people. Titus was prohibited from holding his annual procession in honour of the Mother of God. At the last minute the prohibition was withdrawn, but it was too late to reorganize the procession. The study days, set aside for the Apostolate of Reunion, were likewise forbidden. When, at Christmas 1940, Professor Hoogveld returned from prison Titus met a broken man.

The long corridors in the Priory were dark in the evening as it was not possible to blackout every window; and a number of apartments remained unused. The darkness inside was bleak and depressing; outside it would occasionally flare into a

As a young Carmelite

Nijmegen: the photograph on the left shows Brandsma's signature. The photograph below, taken in his study, is one of the last before his death

terrifying brilliance as searchlights fanned the sky, or, more sombre still, a burning plane spiralled towards the earth.

The Jews were already classified. Titus's old master and friend, Dr Hubertus, had been ill which left him partly paralyzed. With his left hand he typed a few lines to Titus. Both agreed: they must show patience in all things.

The University suffered a great loss in the death of an eminent jurist, shortly after two of Titus's sisters had died. More than once that year he was to speak about death as the road to union with God. He was, however, not the sort of man to seek suffering deliberately. He was not among those mystics who specifically offer themselves to God as a victim. Liduina had done so and somewhere Titus remarked that 'she had been warned that God sometimes accepts such offerings'.

On Passion Sunday, 1939, hardly three months after her escape from Germany to Holland, the Carmelite nun, Edith Stein, had offered herself 'for the sake of true peace'. Earlier on, she had already expressed her willingness to become a sacrifice for her people. This sensitive, intelligent Jewess, who certainly surpassed Titus Brandsma as a creative philosopher, was one of those who were to be asked to play her hand in the way in which she had called it. But Titus seemed to prefer otherwise. He always maintained a cautious and reserved attitude towards anything extraordinary or extreme. As spiritual director, his preference seems to have tended towards a radical acceptance of what Ida Görres called the 'accidental suffering' and, even then, only when convinced that it is destined for him. The petition he drew up in the prison at Kleve shows this, though he did not keep God waiting once he knew what was in store for him.

Titus himself had no illusions. In Germany, the eyes of many had been opened when it was too late. But Titus knew the system. Shortly before the war, he had lectured for a whole year on National Socialism, pointing out its fallacies with realistic acumen, but adding that one should never react with hatred. Love for the people who had been tricked must always confound hatred, our hatred.[67] This comment had been looked upon as theory, but with Professor Brandsma theory usually turned into practice.

When, in the autumn of 1935, marriage laws against the Jews were announced at Nuremberg, Titus Brandsma wrote a protest to the Press. The Berlin paper *Fridericus* reacted with a taunting article. Hardly a year later a paper of the Nationalist Socialist Movement in Nijmegen accused Brandsma of sympathizing with the communists. In 1939, another periodical attacked both the Archbishop of Utrecht and Dr Brandsma, realizing that the Nazi movement would find staunch opponents in them.

After the occupation, the Jews, the Press, and those in charge of education became the Nazis' immediate targets. It was then that Titus became a close colleague of the Archbishop of Utrecht, who frequently consulted him. The association brought him into contact with the Protestant leaders as well as with the new regime. This happened just at the time when the prohibition that 'priests and religious are not to be nominated rector, director, or head of an institution of education in the widest sense of the word' came into being. They were to be dismissed, at the latest, by the 1st May, 1941. The regime also decided to withdraw sixty per cent of the salaries of those who lived in a religious community, thereby making it nearly impossible for schools run by religious orders to carry on.

It was the moment, moreover, when the Church in Holland was to be confronted with the issue of children of Jewish origin who were receiving a Catholic education. Titus received special powers from the Catholic Education Council to thrash these matters out, provided he kept in contact with all concerned and told them at every stage exactly what was happening. He travelled up and down the country trying to mitigate the Nazi sentence and to make it known to the occupying power that 'the Church in carrying out her mission makes no distinction between sex, race, or people'.

He was pleased that his efforts weren't altogether in vain though he wondered how long these results would last. It is difficult, at this stage, to be quite sure about the measures he took and the methods he adopted as we know practically nothing about the documents which the Sicherheitspolizei took away when they arrested Titus in January 1942 and it is unlikely that we shall ever discover exactly what was happening that previous autumn. However, there is one known document that viewed the possiblity of taking Jews to Brazil. It is clear that Titus was considering the prospect of removing them to safety in the Carmelite monasteries out there. Little else has been put on paper. Perhaps it was better that way. At this stage the regime tried to get control of the Press, radio, and education by all possible means of persuasion rather than by brute violence. Such was the picture of Holland under the Nazis in 1941.

In spite of constant political pressure, Titus was not immune to the more familiar requests from nearer home. Someone reminded him that an article for the Apostolate of Reunion was badly needed. But Titus's reply suggests that, for once, he was unable to oblige as a matter of grave urgency prevented it. And yet, though on this occasion he excused himself, other people's problems and minor cares continued to receive his whole-hearted attention.

For some months he had been receiving constant letters from members of a Swiss Protestant fraternity which had established itself in the north of Holland. They had been to see him more than once. 'We are glad,' one letter remarked, 'that God's Providence brought us into contact with you.' They expressed their sadness about the devastating war and the division between Christians. Titus had promised to do something for them. They would like to speak to him on the 21st November. Could they? It is possible that Titus managed to combine a visit to them with his trip to a nearby town where the spiritual care of people in labour camps demanded his immediate attention.

Another letter, dated during his last few weeks of liberty, shows us a widow thanking him for all he had done to get her son out of a German prison. 'I thought Professor Brandsma would help,' she said later. 'I don't know how often I went to him for encouragement.' But she didn't make her journey to Nijmegen in vain. In fact it was Titus's appeal to General Christiansen which finally resulted in eight months' grace for the widow's son. When he was released and arrived at Nijmegen on his journey home, Titus was there to welcome him, after which his first thought was to telephone the widowed mother about her son's safety.[68]

Perhaps this is an appropriate moment to pause and face the fact that Titus was approaching his own imprisonment and that these were his last days of freedom. On New Year's Eve 1941, he wrote to his brother Henry, the Franciscan, who was going through a bad phase of nerves. 'The Lord grant you joy above all. Try to live calmly and be relaxed; have full confidence in God, come what may, for He is always with us. Give yourself up quietly to His Providence.'

That same morning, Titus had been with the Archbishop. The two men, both of whom came from the very north of Holland, had together taken a decision that, although they did not know it, was to decide the end of Titus's life.[69]

In the years to come, Archbishop De Jong was often to recall that morning when Titus sat there in the Archbishop's study on the first floor of the house at the Maliebaan in Utrecht. He was there to discuss the order that had just been issued by the Nazis concerning the Catholic Press which obliged them to accept advertisements on behalf of the National Socialist Movement. Titus had not been taken by surprise. Even before the war broke out he had asked a newly-appointed director to a Catholic paper whether he realized what he was taking on, for 'when Hitler invades it won't be so simple'. When the invasion became a reality, he knew that his own position as Spiritual Adviser was a dangerous one and that the consciences of editors and journalists alike were about to be put to the test. As the Nazi intentions became clear, grave issues presented themselves.

At a meeting in Utrecht on the 10th August, 1940, the two existing national Press organizations were considering the possibility of a merger to forestall a move on the part of the Nazis who were planning to replace certain directors by ones who were sympathetic to the new regime. On that day, too, Titus had sat in the study of the Archbishop. In fact he had left the meeting at least three times to go and see the Archbishop. Naturally if there was to be a fusion of the two Press organizations, agreement had to be reached on matters of principle.

At one stage during the meetings Titus became extremely worried that he might not be able to draw the line where his conscience told him it should be drawn. He turned to the chairman of the Press meeting and, with deep emotion, told him that he might feel bound to resign as their Spiritual Adviser. In fact it was Titus himself who actually succeeded in bringing them into an agreement which fully respected the Catholic conscience. He was delighted when he could tell Dr J. De Jong this and return to the meeting with the message that the Archbishop gave his blessing to the proposed merger. Before the year was out, however, the Nazis had dismantled the merger and Titus had to face new complications.

On various occasions during the year that followed (1941) Titus discussed matters with the Archbishop. Details of those private talks are lacking but, perhaps, something can be guessed from the description the Archbishop gave five years later: 'As long as I live, I shall have the figure of Father Brandsma before my eyes. I always admired him, especially during the war, for his courage and clear vision. I asked repeatedly for his advice.' Unfortunately there are no details of these important talks except about the last and crucial discussions of the 31st December, 1941. Both the Archbishop and Titus referred to it later. It was the meeting that decided Titus's fate and about which the Archbishop was led to remark frequently: 'I consider him a martyr.'

The constant refusal to print Nazi propaganda had, by then, become an issue of the gravest importance. It was not possible to print Nazi propaganda and still claim to be a Catholic publication. It had become a clear case of conscience. While the Nazi threat was hanging above the heads of the directors, Titus had been going round trying to find out where his men stood at this critical hour. He had done so at the request of the Archbishop, and, on New Year's Eve, he had reported back.

Aware of his own responsibility as Spiritual Adviser, Titus agreed to the decision that he was to act on behalf of the whole Dutch Hierarchy and deliver a mandate. This was to inform the editors that it was quite impossible to meet the Nazi demands and still remain a Catholic publication.

On New Year's Eve he wrote letters to all the Catholic papers. But he did not send them out. He wrote them in his new study which had recently been added to the Priory building, and that same evening, no doubt, he reflected a little on the year that had come to an end. He did not post the letters at once because he had decided to deliver them personally and explain their points and importance.

On New Year's Day he stayed at home. At the reception, later that day, for the Rector Magnificus he met Mr Bodewes, the director of the provincial paper *De Gelderlander*, who became the first one to learn the news. Titus had prepared his itinerary carefully. Express letters had gone out already to the Bishops, informing them of his coming visits. On Friday morning, the 2nd January, he left by train for Haarlem. He carried his letters with him.

'The limit is reached.' Brandsma's message was crystal clear and he went in person to make it clearer still. Would they listen to him? What would the Nazis do if they did?

Chapter Nine

ON TRIAL

Titus undertook his journey in his capacity as Spiritual Adviser to the Union of Journalists. As he had emphasized in the letters which he was now going to deliver in all parts of the country, it was precisely in this capacity that he saw himself 'obliged' to speak out.

'The Hierarchy acknowledges that as long as editors and directors strive to maintain the specific Catholic character of their paper,' he wrote, 'their striving deserves respect and acknowledgement. But however difficult it may be to draw the line, and however uncertain the extent to which one may go under pressure, there is no doubt that the order which was issued a few days ago by the leading elements in the Press makes the carrying out of such an order a definite infringement on Catholic principles. This is the order which forces editors to accept advertisements from the National Socialist Movement and which explicitly states that refusal on grounds of principle is not tolerated. The leaders themselves are hereby deliberately making an issue out of a principle. Catholic papers cannot comply. The order has not yet been made official. The papers have received the instruction via the telex. It is possible that it will not be made official. So much the better. But, if it should happen or if such advertisements as referred to by the telex instruction were placed, the directors and editors must refuse their publication if they value the Catholic character of their newspapers even though they are threatened with a fine or suspension, or, worse, with the liquidation of the paper concerned.

'We have reached the limit. I trust that, in this matter, the Catholic newspapers will maintain the Catholic position. The more firmly everyone follows the same line, the stronger they will be.

'You will understand,' Titus continued, 'that I am only writing after mature consideration and consultation with colleagues as well as with the Archbishop. The management of the papers may be informed about our position. If they do not acknowledge it they will make it impossible for the Catholic newspapers to continue. Even if they continue to exist in the material sense, they will no longer be able to count on Catholic readers and subscribers to support them. They will die without honour.

'The decision is a hard one for many who, up to now, have been honourably and rewardingly employed. The responsibility rests with those who, in spite of all their promises, do violence to the consciences of directors and editors. As yet, I find it hard to believe that the authorities will go so far as this. But, if they do, God will have the last word and will reward the faithful servant.'

When Bishop Huibers of Haarlem met Titus and learnt of his mission, he, like the Archbishop, pointed out to Titus that, from now on, he himself was in danger. To this Titus reacted calmly. When he left, he asked for the Bishop's blessing. Bishop Huibers never forgot that brief visit.

From there Titus went further on by train to meet a chief editor and managing director, then back again to Amsterdam's Central Station where he met others. Next day found him with the Bishops of Den Bosh and Breda and with yet more editors to whom he had still to deliver his letter.

On Sunday, the 4th January, he was at Nijmegen. Here he received a visit from a Jesuit who emphasized his own conviction that the times required that priests and laity should work hand in hand. Titus agreed, adding that priests had to share the carrying of their burden and responsibility whatever the consequences.[70]

It was a Wednesday, the 7th January, when he took a break and stayed at the Priory in Merkelbeek where he always went with such pleasure. There he could see again the large body of student-friars, his old master, Dr Hubertus, and the rest of the Community, with whom he was glad to join in the official recitation of the Divine Office.

When he arrived at Merkelbeek, Titus had already visited fourteen newspapers. His visits included one to a man who had already taken the wrong turn. To him Titus simply said: 'In the eyes of many you are a hopeless case. But I did not want to pass you by, for I never doubted that you were in good faith.'

After Titus's arrest this particular person felt very isolated, for no one, including the Archbishop, thought it worthwhile bothering with him.

Meanwhile, the name Brandsma was being mentioned in The Hague. The Nazi, Willy Janke, who was in charge of Press affairs, dictated on the 7th January a memorandum to the Generalkommissar, Herr Schmidt, one of the four close collaborators of Seyss-Inquart, requesting the immediate arrest of Father Brandsma. He was simultaneously listed as a candidate for a concentration camp.

Someone had betrayed Titus. The enemy knew the contents of his letter and the details of his recent journeys. Janke even knew that, when Father Brandsma would have completed his journeys and received a guarantee of loyalty from all the Catholic papers, he, Janke, would receive a visit from the director of the Catholic newspaper *De Tijd* who would inform him that, were the Nazi order enforced, their newspapers would cease to be a Catholic medium of information. Furthermore, Janke knew that, in case Father Brandsma did not succeed in obtaining a pledge of loyalty from all the Catholic newspapers, the Hierarchy would write a pastoral letter in which they would call upon their people to withdraw their subscriptions.

On Thursday, the 8th January, Titus set out again on his travels, unaware of the impending Nazi threat. His fellow monks prayed that he might succeed. Then, on Saturday, he went to report back to the Archbishop.

It was dark when the two great men met for the last time. There was much at stake. Men's livelihoods and their lives were on trial as well as their faith. They needed reassurance and support. Some of those Titus had visited had requested a letter from the Hierarchy. The Archbishop understood their needs very well and asked Titus to draw up a draft which he could place before the other Bishops. It is not improbable that Titus did this that same evening and left it with the Archbishop before he departed. Ironically, only a few hundred feet from the Archbishop's house another meeting was taking place that same evening.

The V.I.P.s from the National Socialist Movement conferred together to decide not to place advertisements in the Catholic Press. But, by this time, it was too late for the decision to affect Brandsma's fall. Already his betrayer had taken prompt action. But he had been observed by someone on Titus's side. Only a few days ago somebody had called on the Prior at Nijmegen. He had travelled there solely to give the Prior a warning. Professor Brandsma must go into hiding. They were after him. Undeterred, Titus presided over the profession of a member of the third Order. It was going to be a year of horror, he had remarked that evening. He had appeared to his audience to be gravely concerned but everyone noticed how naturally and humourously he mingled with the people afterwards.

Did someone that evening tell him about the visit of that stranger? We do not know, but we do know that the following Sunday, when he went to see a member of the Press in the west of Holland, he knew that the enemy was well informed. 'The Germans are after me,' he said. 'They are saying that I am committing sabotage. They don't understand at all. But I am going to carry on. Let them arrest me.'

The way Titus had said it clearly showed that he realized what it would mean. After more travelling, Titus returned to the Priory at Merkelbeek. It was decided that he should not show himself for the time being at Nijmegen. In the meanwhile the Archbishop was preparing a letter to tell him that the Hierarchy had accepted his draft for the letter that was to be sent to all the newspapers. The Archbishop had added a postscript to the effect that he had received, and agreed with, Titus's request to wait on account of certain dubious indications from the enemy.

But, late one evening, before Titus had received the Archbishop's letter, the telephone rang at Merkelbeek. When Titus picked up the receiver he heard, at the other end of the line, the voice of the Archbishop telling him that delay was no longer possible. He had just learnt that three Catholic papers had been sent a particularly eye-catching Nazi advertisement. Titus listened and agreed. They said good-bye. At Utrecht and at Merkelbeek they put down the receivers simultaneously.

Their conversation had been short, detached. It was to be their last. On Wednesday, the 14th January, someone who announced himself as a student telephoned the Nijmegen Priory from Arnhem and asked whether Professor Brandsma was in.

'No,' replied the brother who answered the call, 'I am afraid not.'

Was it possible to get the Professor by telephone? the other asked, his manner polite, solicitous.

The brother hesitated and replied that he didn't know.

When would the Professor be back then?

In answer to this question the brother suggested that the caller should try again on Sunday.

At Merkelbeek Titus carried on with his correspondence as if nothing unusual were happening. He realized that his days were numbered and he had already ruled out the possibility of going into hiding. The men whose Spiritual Adviser he was had to stay firm. What effect would it have were he suddenly to disappear himself? At the Priory he made certain arrangements and entrusted a confidential matter to Dr Cyrillus. When people touched on the danger he was in, Titus remarked with a gay twinkle: 'Now I am going to get what has so seldom been my lot, and what I have always wanted: a cell of my own. Now at last I shall be a real Carmelite.'

On Saturday, Titus returned to Nijmegen. By Sunday he had already left again for the town of Oldenzaal to deal with matters concerning the Apostolate for Reunion. At Oldenzaal, the Carmelites ran a lyceum which was attended by an Armenian orphan by the name of Michael Polatian who had become Titus's 'protégé'. The boy's parents had escaped from the Turkish terror into Greece where he was born. To make sure that he was well provided for, Titus went to see the family

Michael was staying with. When he left them, he turned around a few times to wave good-bye with his hat.

It was bitterly cold. He walked quickly along the winding road to the station. He broke the journey at Utrecht and thought of calling upon the Archbishop. Jule, the housekeeper, answered the door but she looked dismayed. The Archbishop had just gone for a long walk. When he heard this, Titus decided to go back to the station to catch the next train to Amsterdam.

When the Archbishop returned and heard who had called he was upset beyond measure. He was unable to put into words the regret he felt on learning that he had missed Titus; they had been so close to seeing one another.

That same afternoon two men called at the Nijmegen Priory. The younger of the two introduced himself as a student and asked for Professor Brandsma, but Titus was on his way to Amsterdam to see a rather jovial priest friend who was also in the Apostolate for Reunion. He wished to discuss with him the future well-being of his Armenian orphan. Later on, the curates of the parish joined them and together they relaxed. The following morning, Monday the 19th January, Titus said Mass for the last time in his life. He said it in the heart of Amsterdam, in the church dedicated to the memory of St Boniface. He then said good-bye to his host. Possibly they may have recalled that the intention of that day in the Unity Octave was about reunion with Christians in the East.

From there, Titus went to The Hague to confer with the authorities in the Department of Education. It is not known where he went for lunch. From The Hague he went back to Nijmegen. The train was over-crowded and he had to stand. Someone recognized him and they exchanged a few words. At four o'clock in the afternoon he was at the University to give his first lecture since the Christmas holidays. To the students he seemed his usual humourous self. But perhaps they, too, would reflect later on the subject of his lecture that evening – the meaning of history.

Chapter Ten

A HOTEL IN SCHEVENINGEN (CELL 577)

It was about six o'clock on the 19th January, when the two men who had called the previous day made their second appearance. The brother who answered the door led them to the parlour and told Titus of their return. After a few moments' conversation with them, Titus led them to his new study. Time dragged on. There was little sound from within. Twice, without getting any answer, the brother knocked on the door, once for a telephone call and once for a visitor. Still no reply. He was worried. He stood anxiously outside the door. Someone inside could be overheard speaking in German. He told a colleague, a friar who was working in a room next to the study, and the friar listened too. Suddenly he was convinced that he heard the word *Sicherheitspolizei*. He left his room in search of the Prior.

When the latter hurried along the passage he saw Titus, followed by another man, going into his bedroom. The door was shut behind them. After a moment the Prior knocked and, without waiting for a reply, went in.

'This gentleman of the Sicherheitspolizei has come to arrest me,' Titus said, introducing a good-looking young man who stood gazing down at a paper on the desk. His name, he explained, was Steffen. It was not the first time he had been seen in Nijmegen. The Prior asked boldly for the reason of the arrest. He was told that it was none of his business.

Titus tried to tell the Prior something about a document that urgently needed finishing. But the Sicherheitspolizei placed his hand on Professor Brandsma's arm. The document must stay there. He had been given every chance to find it. He had been very lenient, but now his time was up. The Prior was told to leave. Titus knelt down and asked the young friar who was his Superior for his blessing. He then changed his religious habit for a black suit. Meanwhile, a detective had arrived to seal off the room. Steffen was in a hurry. He wanted to catch the 6.35 p.m. train for Arnhem.

In Titus's study the other 'visitor', a Dutchman, filled a suitcase with books and papers. Titus was calm and helpful. With the Prior and Steffen's assistant beside him, he went to the front door.

Steffen arranged the final details about the inspection process with the detective as several friars gathered around the front door. They were deeply moved by the Professor's departure.

'Memento mei,' he said.

Then he looked at his watch and remarked that Steffen should hurry if he wanted to catch the train as railways don't wait for anyone.

Just as they were leaving, the director of a Catholic newspaper rang the doorbell. Someone opened the door and Titus, seeing who was there, said: 'I am afraid we can't keep our appointment. I am under arrest.'

They greeted each other and then, walking between Steffen and his assistant, Titus was taken to a car that stood waiting for them further down the road. Outside there was a severe frost, but they were just in time to catch the train.

Titus spent the night on a straw mattress in a prison cell in Arnhem. He did not sleep. The following morning he was taken by train to The Hague.

Someone who saw him on the platform in Arnhem noticed how calm he seemed in his black suit with the decoration on the left lapel. On the 31st August, 1939, the last time that Holland had celebrated the birthday of Queen Wilhelmina in freedom, he had been honoured with the high decoration of Knight in the Order of Oranje Nassau. He was not handcuffed but the person who tried to greet him was seized by the collar and pulled aside.

Scheveningen, near The Hague, was his destination. He was to be there for seven weeks in what had once been the Oranje Hotel. But the Germans had taken every conceivable measure to convert a normally comfortable hotel into a proper prison. Stripped of whatever luxury it may previously have had, it provided prisoners with a series of small bleak cells (as the photograph on page   shows).

Through the window, high above the door of his cell, Titus could only see the sky, although, as he wrote to Nijmegen, 'now and then a seagull passes.' He did not have long to watch it when it did for his window was generally frosted over except for the one or two hours a day when the meagre sun demisted it for him, for the winter of 1942, when he occupied cell 577 in Scheveningen, was a severe one.

Referring to the conflicting principles of the Nazis and Catholicism which had caused his arrest, he wrote a few days later: 'The opposition of the principles is there. I suffer with joy what has to be suffered for sticking to one's principles. My vocation to the Church and to the priesthood has given me so much that is wonderful that I am equally pleased to take up something unpleasant. So far it is not so bad. And though I don't know what is to happen, I put myself entirely in God's hands. *Quis me separabit a caritate Dei?* (Who shall separate me from the love of God?).'[71]

The endless questioning was over. When he had entered the prison at Arnhem he had jokingly told Steffen that it felt odd to be sent to prison at the age of sixty, to which Steffen had retorted that he could have spared himself this had he not accepted the order of the Archbishop. Rather encouraged by Steffen's remark, he told him while they went inside 'to consider it an honour'.[72]

When he arrived at Scheveningen he found he was an unexpected guest. No arrangements had been made for him, although he was given some bread as they had telephoned through that he had not yet eaten. He got a jug with water, a towel, another small cloth, and two blankets. Because of his late arrival the light in his cell was kept on a little longer before being switched off by the authorities.

He was told that questioning in The Hague would be resumed next day and he could then, in all probability, return home. So when a young fellow prisoner turned up next morning with a sheet, Titus told him that he had come too late as he would be going home that day. The young man advised him to take it all the same. He had been told the same story when he had been locked up! So it could not have come altogether as a surprise to Titus to learn, some hours later, that the Germans wished to keep him in prison, and under arrest, for a longer period of 'clarification'.

The first night, without a sheet, he had felt a little unenthusiastic about the straw mattress and blankets, and had kept his socks on. And as he could not bear the prickling of the blanket he had folded his towel under and over the top of him.

Every time he was questioned Titus was taken to the Headquarters of the Sicherheitspolizei which occupied the Ministerial buildings of the Dutch Government in The Hague. There Hauptscharführer Hardegen dealt with Group IV, which was responsible for Church affairs. Group III A 3 was concerned with the Press, and both groups wanted to take Brandsma's case. An argument arose but Hardegen was determined. He had already made his arrangement and would deal with the case himself.

Titus had never heard of Hardegen,[73] but during the first week he was to have several long conversations with the tall, blond German who was always so assiduously courteous to him. Hardegen was not a man to run through a list of prepared questions that someone else had briefed him with. He used his own intelligence and asked his own questions. These followed their own logic, running in front of, and behind, Brandsma's answers, leading suavely from one conclusion to the next.

Towards the end of a particularly long interrogation, the Carmelite priest repeated once more that his activity in regard to the Press had been his grave duty for it had been a protest on religious grounds directed against a system which was in conflict with Christianity. In a separate interview he stated this even more precisely, explaining that faith makes any sacrifice possible. Hardegen, mentally on his toes as always, came back with the quick reply: 'And as the Church knows of this attitude among her members, is she now trying to sabotage the orders of the occupying power and so endanger the interior

peace of the country and prevent the National Socialist
Weltanschauung?'

Titus replied coolly, almost matter-of-factly: 'The Catholic
Church in Holland follows the ordinances of the occupying
power in so far as it is not in direct disagreement with the principles of the Catholic Church. Where it becomes a matter of
conscience, however, the Church must refuse to collaborate,
whatever the consequences may be. If one of the consequences
is to destroy a nation's peace of mind, the Church deeply
regrets it. But she cannot refuse to act her part because of it.
The National Socialist ideas are being fought by the Church
on grounds of *Weltanschauung* and religion.'

Towards the end of another interview he said: 'When
measures are taken which are irreconcilable with Catholic
teaching, the Church is obliged to refute them. I am told that
I am under arrest until this affair has been cleared up. But one
thing I must make clear: the attitude of the Dutch Hierarchy
is my own.'

Hardegen's constant intention was to place everything
under the heading of sabotage.

Father Brandsma was not like those legendary martyrs who
ran eagerly towards their 'palm of martyrdom'. He did his best to
remain alive so long as it was honourably possible to do so
and he worked on several arguments which might be used in
his favour. He was essentially a realistic man who saw little
point in volunteering himself for death if living would prove
more useful. He made a similar attempt to cool down the
atmosphere when he was staying in the transitory prison of
Kleve in Germany. It was from there that he wrote a petition
on grounds of his delicate health for a different sort of arrest,
even suggesting to those who might listen that he could be
safely placed under house arrest in a German monastery. He
did this although he knew he had not much of a case, that his
'informing' activities were known to entail much more than
merely delivering a message from the Hierarchy.

He had even boldly admitted to Hardegen that he would
not act differently were he to find himself in a similar situation
again.[74] Some fuss has been made about the word 'mandate'.

Among the Catholics in Holland there were those who interpreted it to mean that the Archbishop of Utrecht had compelled Father Brandsma. In doing so they gave too rigid a meaning to the word. The Archbishop had chosen it for want of a better one; it had struck him as apt for the occasion. The relationship between Archbishop De Jong and Titus Brandsma, moreover, and especially the atmosphere of their discussions, rules out any possibility of interpreting the word 'mandate' in a compulsory sense.

Commenting on the controversy among the Catholics, Dr De Jong said: 'Bishops have broad shoulders. I made that quite clear to him (Titus). On the one hand it speaks for Father Brandsma's courage that he did what he did. On the other hand, he regarded it as *his* duty as Spiritual Adviser to do so.'

The same question came up during the process of beatification, when the Vice-Postulator asked the Archbishop if the Professor had acted in his own name or on the authority of the Hierarchy; Dr De Jong replied with absolute confidence that he had acted in his own name. 'Moreover,' he went on to explain, 'there were different opinions among the men of the Press as to what was permissible and what was not, and Father Brandsma was "the" man to clarify our directives.'

To others the Archbishop remarked that even if the Bishops (instead of Brandsma) had voiced the same decisive views, he would still have been arrested, for the Nazis knew 'that both of us were responsible'. He made no secret of the fact that he himself valued Titus Brandsma more highly than any of his other advisers. Dr Jan De Jong, that great figure of the war period in Holland who so often hid his sensitiveness behind a barrier of scepticism, once remarked to Titus's Prior with the murmured regret: 'I should never have let him go.'

Titus himself never for an instant misunderstood the Archbishop's motives. In the first letter he wrote after his arrest, his first thought was for the man at Maliebaan in Utrecht: 'Will you tell Dr De Jong that he must not worry about me or reproach himself in any way.'

The documents and accompanying letter which the Sicherheitspolizei forwarded to Berlin indicated clearly that Father

Brandsma had been arrested, and must be detained, on account of his activities in regard to the Catholic Press. It must, therefore, have come as a surprise to a distant relative of Titus when, on the 2nd April, he called upon Hardegen and tried, in his capacity as a lawyer, to achieve something for Titus. Hardegen, polite as always, simply didn't mention the Press affair. The reasons he gave for Titus's incarceration were very different. It looks as if he and his colleagues conspired to conceal from the general public the real cause behind Brandsma's arrest. Hardegen referred to Titus's protest against the Nazi policy towards the Jews; he accused him of being principally anti-National Socialistic and of having disseminated his prejudices as widely as possible.

When a little later, in June, the Prior of Nijmegen called upon him with the same aim, Hardegen repeated similar accusations. Were the Nazis shaken by the number and strength of the arguments put forward on Brandsma's behalf and were they reconsidering their decision and his fate? If so, it would then be politic to avoid bringing their real motives into the open. Or were these accusations simply trumped up to prevent Brandsma from being acknowledged a martyr for the Catholic Faith? At any rate the position remained unchanged.

Meanwhile, the secret police in Berlin received the documents which accused Titus Brandsma of having seriously undermined the ordinances of the German force in Holland through his activities in the Catholic Press. Fortunately, the text of the interrogation with Hardegen and his conclusion in an accompanying letter to the Berlin Headquarters, have been preserved. In addition, any uncertainty that might still exist as to the real grounds for Titus's arrest are immediately dispelled by the German document *Jahresbericht 1942* which appeared in the *Meldungen aus den Niederlanden*, a stencilled publication of 1943 and marked: 'Secret'.

It states that, in Holland in 1942, two hundred and thirty-eight executions took place and that the Sicherheitspolizei had taken action against *rund 10,000 Niederländer* – 'about ten thousand Dutchmen'. It then becomes apparent how very strongly the Nazis had felt about the Press activities of Titus Brandsma who, by January 1943, had already been dead for six months. Let the Germans speak for themselves: 'Apart from the readings from the pulpits of pastoral letters and messages directed against National Socialism and the N.S.B. (the Dutch Nazi party), the Catholic clergy, in the beginning of 1942, attempted a great Press campaign against the N.S.B. . . . The prompt action of the Sicherheitspolizei, and the arrest of Professor Brandsma, *des führenden Kopfes dieser aktion* (the leading man in this matter), defeated this attempt at the outset.'

Further on, on page 64, under the heading 'Press' one reads: 'At the beginning of the year under review (namely the year 1942), the proposed National Socialist reorganization in every department gave the signal to the religious denominations for a particularly strong movement in the field of the Press. The Catholic Church assigned to her opposition the most able and well-tried adviser of the R.C. Union for journalists, Professor Brandsma.' The same article goes on to say that the Catholic opposition had been well thought out and that the Catholic Church had counted for its effectiveness on her prohibition of the National Socialist movement. The article concludes by saying: 'Brandsma was arrested and the systematic activity, already begun, suppressed.'[75]

The small Carmelite priest was thus acknowledged in the German corridors of power to be the chief opponent of all attempts to impose a Godless and materialistic way of life upon the Dutch Catholics.

On the evening of the 21st January, Hardegen had told Titus that his arrest was to be prolonged for the purpose of further 'clarification'. He was left in his cell and asked to give a written reply to the question: 'Why does the Dutch Nation, especially its Catholic populations, oppose the N.S.B.' For this purpose he was given plenty of paper, ink, and a pen. Some of the paper he used for another purpose, to write his cell memoirs which, together with all his other belongings, were sent to Nijmegen after his death. In the Dutch edition these memoirs amount to twenty-four printed pages.

Not only do these memoirs give us an account of life in the

political prison established in the Oranje Hotel at Scheveningen, but they also afford us an insight into the soul of Titus Brandsma. During his stay there from the 20th January to the 12th March, he was twice allowed to write a letter. Both of these were addressed to the Priory at Nijmegen, and dated respectively 18th February and 5th March. We will return to them shortly.

Titus was still allowed to smoke and was given back his watch. As his watch had stopped he had to guess what hour it might be. 'I have therefore my own time, independent of Greenwich, Amsterdam or Berlin,' he wrote in his memoirs, as humourously as ever. His breviary had not been taken from him when he arrived. So he decided to open it at the page illustrating the Madonna of Carmel by Freiin von Oer and place it on the small top shelf above his bed. 'At my table I only have to look a little to the right and I have her image before me. When I am in bed, my eye catches at once the star-bearing Madonna, *Spes omnium Carmelitarum* (the Hope of all Carmelites).'[76]

On his desk he had put a picture of the Crucified Christ, by fra Angelico. In Spanish he wrote out St Teresa's famous words: 'Let nothing disturb thee, Let nothing affright thee, All passeth away, God alone abideth. Patience obtaineth all things. He who hath God can want for nothing, God alone sufficeth.' And in German: 'God so near and far, God is always there' (St Teresa).[77]

Having discovered a few pins, he put these words up on a draughts board which he also found in his cell, to comfort and sustain him. No doubt they did so as he sat down to think out his answer to Hardegen's questionnaire.

He made no attempt to dissemble; casuistry had no attraction for him. He did not hesitate to reply to Hardegen's questions with astounding honesty. The charming Titus, who had moved so many by his goodness and lightness of touch, had little difficulty in being honest. He favoured the direct approach. Some of his confrères couldn't understand that he could speak his mind in such a direct manner when he thought that something wasn't quite right. They thought it a shortcoming, especially when he had to criticize things while no longer a Prior. Perhaps they were right.

But it was with the same straightforwardness that he replied to Hardegen's questions now. Without any reference books he quoted from a German publication. In considerable detail he worked out the differences between the two countries in terms of psychology, character, intelligence, and productivity. He tried to show how clumsily the Germans acted in trying to impose their system upon another nation. He got down to the religious aspect and wrote that the Dutch people, out of love for God, have made great sacrifices in the course of history; that Protestants as well as Catholics have numerous martyrs whom they haven't forgotten and who will inspire them to withstand any suppression of their faith. He did not shrink from pointing out, and Hardegen's question necessitated it, that the Catholics had traditions 'which are their glory and honour. Untold numbers have given up their positions, possessions, families, and even lives during the centuries of persecution. In these days, when religious ties are certainly no less strong where they concern the majority of the Dutch people, it will be no different. The suppression of the religious ecclesiastical influence is not only an offence to God in relation to His creatures, but a violation of the glorious traditions of the Dutch people. Herein lies the heart of the matter.'

And it is here that Titus wrote, in the plainest possible terms, of the 'far-going arrogance and gross incompetence' of Party members who had got into high position and alienated all those who came into contact with them. 'On the one hand, the Dutch people laugh because of their inflated conceit and shrug off their influence with a shrug of their shoulders; on the other hand, they view it with indignation, but especially with concern, since they regard it as a dangerous symptom of meddling with a nation's interest.'

With this, Brandsma came out into the middle of the arena, for his complaint was openly and directly addressed to the oppressor and as such deserves a place along with the classic letters of Archbishop De Jong and the documents of the Protestant Churches (who at the same time were drawing up a list of grievances and refusals to co-operate) and all those who oppose tyranny.

'God bless The Netherlands,' Titus ended his formal essay in reply to Hardegen. 'God bless Germany. God grant both nations, so akin to each other in many ways, to come together in peace and unity, and to stand next to one another in recognition of God and His honour.'

Hardegen later remarked to one of Titus's relatives: 'He thinks he has to protect Christianity.' He didn't realize that in saying so he paid Titus the highest tribute he could. He conceded that, 'In his (Titus's) firm conviction he truly showed himself a man of character.' Nevertheless his conclusion remained the same: '*Er ist sehr gefährlich*' ('He is very dangerous').

Hardegen brushed aside any argument put forward on the ground of Titus' health, saying that 'he should have considered that when he began to agitate against Germany.' And he added: 'It is not our intention to free him before the end of the war.'

On Titus' evidence, Hardegen treated him with courtesy throughout these severe hours of interrogation, but afterwards he took the same course as other bureaucrats of the regime and delivered him up to the people of the S.S. who ran the concentration camps. There, no time was lost in translating official correctness into horror and humiliation.

For the time being, however, Titus was to remain in the prison at Scheveningen. It is not known whether he saw Hardegen again. Hardegen was already dealing with other cases and had become, curiously in the circumstances, rather forgetful. He even forgot to ask for Titus's written reply to his questionnaire. Later, in the concentration camp at Amersfoort, Brandsma is said to have mentioned this to a fellow prisoner.[78]

But when he returned to Scheveningen, a cell companion saw him at work on it and was told what it was. A copy was then left for the Sicherheitspolizei in The Hague, while Titus kept the other copy.

During his second period at Scheveningen (which dated from the 28th April till the 16th May), Titus appeared more than once before Hardegen but the result was always the same. Hardegen then appeared to remember his request and

asked for a written reply. Titus had lost the copy he had
intended for Hardegen but he still had the first draft which he
now wrote out anew.[79]

During these weeks Titus had no one with whom to share
his prison cell. In the Album that was presented to him in
1939, Regout, his colleague on the professorial staff at Nijmegen
University, had called him 'tranquil and yet restless, a mystic
in the midst of a full life'. Now the restlessness of a full life had
fallen away and what those who were even superficially
acquainted with the man might have predicted, happened:
the mystic tranquillity and fullness overflowed and filled up
the emptiness.

'*Beata solitudo*' . . . he wrote in his memoirs, 'I am completely
at home in this little cell. I haven't been bored once. On the
contrary, I am alone, yes, but never has the good Lord been
so near to me. I could shout for joy that He has allowed Himself
to be found by me, without me meeting people or people (being
allowed to meet) me. He is now my sole refuge and I feel safe
and happy. I am willing to remain here always, if He will
allow me to. Rarely have I been so happy and content.'

It was about this time that the future Colonel Fogtelo
accompanied the prison barber along the corridor from cell to
cell. Fogtelo had belonged to the resistance movement and had
been taken prisoner. Some of the prisoners had been given
certain tasks within the prison walls and Fogtelo had been
allotted the duty of accompanying such persons as the barber
from cell to cell. When Brandsma's cell was opened, Fogtelo
was flabbergasted to see the inmate step forward with a
radiant smile on his face. Fogtelo was only too familiar with
the general atmosphere in the prison, where many committed
suicide that winter.

Who on earth was this man in cell 577? he asked himself.
They could not exchange many words. One had to be careful
to avoid rousing suspicion and say as little as possible if one
did not want to lose what few privileges there were. Each
time he visited Titus he experienced the same radiant greeting.
When the iron door of the cell closed, Fogtelo knew that
behind it there remained a happy man.

Three weeks later Titus expressed his happiness in a poem that became famous throughout Holland. It was composed before the image of the Crucified Christ on his desk. Someone in the prison got hold of a copy, and someone else smuggled it out. It passed from hand to hand and more copies were made, so that long before Titus's own copy (together with all his other belongings) was returned to Nijmegen after his death, the original merely provided confirmation, if confirmation was needed, that Brandsma was the real author of the poem. Here, side by side with the Dutch original, are two English translations of the poem, though the reader will appreciate that in the process of translation much of its original force, if not its poetic effect, is lost.

O Jezus, als ik U aanschouw
Dan leeft weer dan ik van U hou'
En dat ook Uw Hart mij bemint,
Nog wel als Uw bijzondren vrind.

Al vraagt mij dat meer lijdensmoed,
Och, alle lijden is mij goed.
Omdat ik daardoor U gelijk,
En dit de weg is naar Uw Rijk.

Ik ben gelukkig in mijn leed,
Omdat ik dit geen leed meer weet.
Maar 't alleruitverkorenst lot,
Dat mij vereent met U, o God.

Och, laat mij hier maar stil alleen,
Het kil en koud zijn om mij heen,
En laat geen mensen bij mij toe,
't Alleen zijn word ik hier niet moe.

Want Gij, O Jezus, zijt bij mij,
Ik was U nimmer zo nabij,
Blijf bij mij, bij mij, Jezus zoet,
Uw bijzijn maakt mij alles goed.

12th–13th February, 1942.

Dear Lord, when looking up to Thee,
I see Thy loving eyes on me;
Love overflows my humble heart,
Knowing what faithful friend Thou art.

    A cup of sorrow I foresee,
    Which I accept for love of Thee.
    Thy painful way I wish to go;
    The only way to God I know.

My soul is full of peace and light;
Although in pain, this light shines bright.
For here Thou keepest to Thy breast
My longing heart, to find there rest.

    Leave me here freely alone,
    In cell where never sunlight shone,
    Should no one ever speak to me,
    This golden silence makes me free!

For though alone, I have no fear;
Never wert Thou, O Lord, so near.
Sweet Jesus, please, abide with me;
My deepest peace I find in Thee.

(translated by Albert Groeneveld)

JESUS MERELY

Jesus, merely
thinking of you
brings to my love
new warmth.

Your love makes me
— through suffering —
your special friend.

Give me, O Lord,
patience to bear
this hard mysterious proof
of how you care.

You walked through pain
the anvil way that led
into your kingdom –
this road I, too, must tread.

My happiness is merely in knowing
that only in pain is joy –
joy to be near – through nails – to you again.

For when I am alone and cold
I am not lonely, you are near,
nearer than blood is nearer to vein.

Stay with me in my dereliction.
Stay with me, Jesus, for when you are near
even my pain is joy for me to bear.

(translated by Ralph Wright, O.S.B.)

It seemed strange language for a social figure, at whose door everyone had been so welcome and who had met every demand without a trace of reserve. But now that he was no longer in need of people he had not forgotten them. He carried their intentions within himself as his letters from prison show.

But Scheveningen betrayed his secret: he had found his true vocation. And it was in the desert of the contemplative hermit, that he made his last retreat.

Cella continuata dulcescit. 'A cell faithfully lived in becomes sweet.' With this quotation from Thomas À Kempis, Titus began his memoirs. He missed his Mass and Communion, but he knew that 'God is nevertheless with me and in me'. To read these pages from prison in their entirety is to be reminded of some of the great writers of the enclosed life, such as Silvio Pellico of his prison, De Maistre of his room.

At first, the prisoner couldn't create any order of the day as he hadn't a clue what might happen next or even what time of day it was. His only clue was that the morning alarm bell rang round about 6.45 a.m. but the prison authorities did not cling to a rigid time-table. Titus decided to draw up his own order of the day which, on the 28th January, he signed with his initials. This, and his letter of the 5th March, show us that his days were filled with prayer.

After a brief morning prayer, he folded the blankets and sheets and placed the jug outside the door which, by that time, had been unlocked. He then said the prayers of the Mass on his knees and made a spiritual communion. It went quicker than usual, he remarked, and added with his typical style of playing on words (which is not apparent in translation), 'but it is also unusual.'

His thoughts went out to Nijmegen when he continued: 'At home meditation comes first, then choir, but here I rather have my Mass first, even though in night attire.' He then washed and dressed in his black suit. 'At about eight o'clock I am again the gentleman, with the exception of my beard, dignified in my black suit and sitting on my stool. As in the monastery I say the Angelus, the Our Father and Hail Mary, and take my breakfast with a spoon.' His memories went back to his Roman days when he went for his holidays to the monastery in Bavaria for 'there we also used to break our bread into the coffee and take it with a spoon.'

After that Titus took his 'morning walk': a few steps to and fro. During the first ten days he still had his pipe and he much appreciated it while he thought 'more fully about the past day and the day that had just begun. I recall many who think of me, and try to live in the *communio Sanctorum* – the communion of Saints.'

Having paced his cell he picked up his breviary which he could now say with much greater leisure than he was normally accustomed to. He did so for half an hour, about the same length of time that he spent on his meditation. For this, he used the book *Jesus* by Cyriel Verschaeve, which he had been allowed to take with him, although at first he was not given it in his cell. Instead he was liberally supplied with novels. 'I had to admit that novels weren't exactly my favoured reading,' he wrote with mild irony, but he was pleased when they exchanged them for an encyclopaedia and a book on the history of art. Both of these he enjoyed. Yet he was glad when the book by Verschaeve and a life of St Teresa by Kwakman were returned to him. 'I now have the things I prefer,' he commented in his memoirs although the pathos of the Flemish writer must have seemed a little contrived in his present circumstances.

As long as he had paper, he wrote from 10–11.30 a.m. Otherwise he read. He was working on a biography of St Teresa of Avila. When he ran out of paper, he found an easy solution. He tore the binding of Verschaeve's book apart and wrote between the lines of its successive pages. On the 5th March he mentioned in a letter that he had completed six of the twelve chapters. A week later he had to break off. He had to stop there, but later on he got another chance to do a little more work on it. The speed with which he worked was considerable. After his death, when all his possessions were returned to the Priory at Nijmegen, there were three hundred and thirty-six closely written pages among them.

He had frequently to improvise for lack of material. He had to make do with Kwakman's adapted work of a book about the *Doctor Mystica*. He wasn't too happy about it, but it was better than nothing. Perhaps in the end, the lack of proper books for his work discouraged him. Certainly his style grew gradually paler and less assured, and he began to express himself with greater difficulty. Dr Brocardus Meyer was later to complete the unfinished work, and he did his best to do so in the spirit of Titus Brandsma so as to preserve the character of the original.

Never before had Brandsma been able to write undisturbed for such a length of time. While walking to and fro, he said 'the little hours' of the Divine Office. The midday meal being over, he knelt 'as in the monastery' to say the Angelus and 'in spirit with his confrères' he made his adoration though, as he noted, he was far from the Eucharistic Presence of Christ. The *Adoro Te* became his beloved prayer. At times he even sang it.

At 2 p.m. he reached again for his breviary. Vespers and compline were followed by the rosary, which he soon postponed till the evening. When he was arrested he had somehow left his rosary behind. He could not understand how he had managed to forget to take it out of his religious habit when he had changed the latter for his black suit.

In his first letter of mid-February he asked for a rosary, the next part of the breviary, a missal and the Latin version of *The Imitation of Christ*. They were quickly dispatched but, in fact, he never got them.

When a relative of his went to see Hardegen, he was told that he could take the things back with him, and so Titus had to remain content with one part of the breviary and his fingers for rosary beads. He used the 'Teresa' edition by Kwakman for his spiritual reading. This took him up to four o'clock when he knelt down on the floor of his cell to meditate for half an hour about 'the life of Jesus and my life'. After supper came the Angelus and, 'in spirit with the monastery', adoration. He either read or wrote till it was eight o'clock. He then said his evening prayers before his bed.

'It doesn't bother me,' he noted in his memoirs, 'if the light is then turned out. I go on praying a little. . . .'

In describing his day, which he carried through methodically as a means of filling in his time, he did not leave out his meals. He wrote about his midday meal appreciatively for, in fact, it was well prepared and by no means unpalatable. Quantity was as good as quality so much so that, as he remarked, 'two-thirds of it is enough for me.'

By the first Thursday morning he had already been visited by the prison doctor and had told him about his physical condition. As a result he was allowed milk that had not been skimmed and a chunk of white bread, which had to do for the evening meal and next morning, instead of the usual brown. Two notices now hung on his cell door: *Milch* (milk) and *Weisbrot* (white bread). On this Titus commented in his memoirs: 'It looks more than it is, but it will do.'

The nights were trying. They were far too long. In Dachau, the position was to be reversed. But here, the light in his cell was switched off round about eight o'clock and it didn't go on until seven next morning. For many years he had been accustomed to only five or six hours of sleep, and it was hard to accustom himself suddenly to eleven hours.

He was able to take a more detached view of prison exercise, which he viewed humourously. Every day, as the cell doors were opened, all the prisoners posted themselves outside their cells along the corridor with their refuse bins. Then they moved off in procession towards the end of the corridor where they left their bins, passed through some more corridors and arrived at an open space behind the prison. High walls concealed it from the outside world. Only the sky above was visible. Then the exercise began; in a wide circle they walked slowly around according to the orders they were given, with high or ordinary steps, the tempo and movements of arms and legs entirely at the discretion of the master of exercises who stood in the centre, as if in a circus ring, egging them on. It did not last long, at the most ten minutes. In the beginning, several prisoners looked curiously at this priest with greying hair in his black overcoat which showed his decoration by the Queen. They watched him sympathetically and occasionally nodded to each other in understanding.

That was all there was to his life in prison as he described it. He had soon measured the walls of his cell and counted the bricks. Later, when he could not get hold of a pair of scissors with which to cut his nails, he tried to do it on the cement floor. 'One has to help oneself,' he commented.

Thursday, the 29th January was the feast of the patron saint of journalists, St Francis de Sales. Ironically, the day was not to end happily for his fellow journalist.

'I had cleaned my pipe especially well and had just lit it for my morning walk,' Brandsma wrote in his memoirs, 'when there came a German soldier with *etwas neues* (some news). I had to hand over my tobacco and cigars, pipe and matches. I was to smoke no more. It was a good thing that I was just thinking about the gentle Francis de Sales, otherwise I might have reacted unkindly. I emptied my pipe and gave him the items he asked for. With obvious sympathy the soldier told me that the order did not come from him. Well, I understood that. To console me he said that I could keep the other things he had brought me: the two books and paper. This was fortunate as they were of more use, however much I missed my pipe and cigar. I struck smoking from my schedule and the day went on as usual. Now, I don't miss it any more. It was certainly a blessing that I was allowed to smoke those first difficult days.'

In Nijmegen, no one had heard from Titus for several weeks. The Prior had arranged that the Brandsma family should address their letters to the Swedish Embassy in Berlin and to the Headquarters of the Sicherheitspolizei in The Hague. But there was no reply. Then the rumour got round that a man had been released who alleged to have seen the professor. The Prior went to visit him and the rumour was confirmed. On the 18th February, to everyone's relief, Titus' first letter, which had been written six days previously, arrived.

Several copies were made and sent round to his relatives and colleagues in other priories. Everywhere they read: 'I am already at home here, I pray, I read, I write, the days are too short. I am very calm, happy and contented.'

He, who was at last totally inaccessible, gave them messages for everyone, from the Archbishop to the Armenian orphan and other students. He also wrote a few lines about a booklet, *The Christian East*, which he had been asked to review and which had been on his desk when they came to arrest him. They should tell the author, he wrote, that his text was a little too gloomy!

In his next letter of the 5th March, it is as if he has to put others at their ease and release them from their concern for him. 'I don't need to weep or to sigh. I even sing now and then, but not, of course, too loud.'

His fellow monks had to smile at this last remark for, at home, Titus often forgot himself when he stood in choir and roared the Divine Office with obvious enjoyment. It had been sometimes disrupting and the Prior had once alluded to it during a Chapter meeting. For some time afterwards Titus had managed to curb his enthusiasm, until he forgot himself again. From his prison cell Titus recalled the occasion and hinted at it mischievously.

In the garden at Nijmegen

The prison cell at Scheveningen

Herr Hardegen, Brandsma's
interrogator at The Hague

The extremely severe winter progressed, as did the Lenten season of the Church, while throughout Europe life became more grim. It must have been sometime during those days that Titus wrote the Stations of the Cross for St Boniface's shrine at Dokkum in Frisia. He wrote them, of course, in prison.

Chapter Eleven

NUMBER 58 – AMERSFOORT

~~~~~~

'The solitude of the cell is over.'

On the Friday before Passion Sunday, 20th March, 1942, a letter dated the 16th March arrived at the Priory in Nijmegen. Four days previously, Titus Brandsma had arrived in the concentration camp at Amersfoort, near Utrecht, officially called: *Polizeiliches Durchgangslager Amersfoort* (P.D.A.). The letter was shorter than the two earlier ones; the style more succinct. It was the voice of a man trying to be brave. On the 12th March several big police cars with canvas covers had driven out of the prison gate at Scheveningen.

At the end of the prison corridor a fellow prisoner had, with his ear against the keyhole of his cell door, listened to the names being called out. As it happened he was Father Van Gestel, the future Assistant-General of the Jesuits. He had occasionally managed to exchange greetings with Titus through a third person. And now, with his ear against the iron door, he had heard the names called out aloud of those who were to leave in the covered trucks. Among them was the name of Brandsma. Titus was one of about a hundred who were to be transported.

Before leaving, each prisoner was allowed to collect his own belongings, including cigarettes, before joining the others in the truck. In no time the van in which Titus found himself was thick with tobacco smoke. A young student passed around a sack of sugar. At first, Titus refused to take any but after some insistence he gladly gave in. It was his first of many future contacts with the young lad called Reef. Elated by the sudden, if momentary, sense of freedom everyone began talking. What kind of spiritual care would they be able to get at their new destination? In Scheveningen, a priest as such had never been seen.[80]

Another priest remarked that to hear confessions would be difficult. 'I won't have any jurisdiction there, I fear.'

Someone asked Titus's opinion. He told them that, 'as we are in an emergency situation, we are after all living in a state of war, we can calmly assume that it is our business to help everyone!'

The man who had put the question felt relieved, and the little group in the van soon became friends.

It must have been around nine o'clock in the evening when the cars turned into the main road and, after driving through thick woods of fir trees, they soon arrived at the gate of the camp. The barrier went up, they had reached their destination. Once again Titus Brandsma was one of the crowd. Everything personal was taken from each prisoner and duly registered. Would Brandsma be allowed to hold on to his breviary? He would be given a different form of breviary, came the reply. The newcomers were kept standing in the cold for several hours while the roll-call was made. It was after midday before the group had been through the formalities and sent off to the clothes shop which was situated outside the fence which surrounded the camp.

A priest, J. Aalders, who had just returned from his camp duty happened to recognize the Professor. Titus had once preached in his parish at Enschede and recognized him too. He waved and smiled. Fortunately no one saw him do this. He still had a lot to learn about what life in the camp was like, but soon it would be made clear to everyone. By this time he had been standing on the frozen snow for several hours, with the temperature several degrees below zero. In the shop, they had to take their clothes off. Then, in groups of ten, the S.S. men drove them outside into the freezing cold. There they stood naked, holding on to the few miserable pieces of clothing that they had been issued. Somebody who had known Titus in Nijmegen was working near the kitchen barracks on the other side of the fence. He called out to him with a coarse laugh. The humiliation was clearly intentional.

When they were at last allowed to dress, Titus put on the old Dutch soldier's uniform with matching cap which everyone had been provided with, together with a pair of wooden shoes. They were allowed to keep small items such as a diary, watch, pen and purse.

No one knows how many prisoners there were in Amersfoort at that time though the numbers are estimated at between six to eight hundred. The population of the camp changed constantly as transports came and went. There were two living quarters in use, both of them with four rooms called 'stuben'. Here, the prisoners slept in bunks, one above the other, on a straw mattress without pillow and sheets, under a couple of worn-out military blankets. Poor Titus – during his first days at Scheveningen he had described how badly he could take 'the tickling' of woollen blankets and that he felt an uncontrollable repugnance to a mattress and blankets without sheets.

In the centre of each room between the rows of bunks, there were a few wooden tables and a stove which was fed with logs which the men of the timber commando had to cut. The SS men had their own coal fire, and occasionally some of the prisoners knew how to get hold of a few lumps. To the right of the camp there was another barracks where the camp doctor resided. Here were the douches and the 'hospital'. Directly opposite was the kitchen, behind which was another 'block' where the dysentery patients were taken. Titus was soon to join them.

Among the prisoners were many men from every walk of life who had belonged to the active resistance organization. There were also several priests and Protestant ministers, with some of whom Titus would establish close contact. The new arrivals, however, had first to learn the routine of the camp. From now on, the only time they would be allowed to change their clothes would be when they had their weekly douche, which they took in a group and without any privacy. There was no longer any point in being embarrassed. After a few days they were only aware of being hungry. The one thing they noticed each Sunday morning, at their douche time, was how rapidly their bodies were losing weight. Titus Brandsma and his companions had arrived in the hell of Amersfoort.

Others have written, in horrifying detail, of what the prisoners in Amersfoort had to endure. Suffice it here to stick to the main essentials. In his first letter from Amersfoort, dated the 16th March in which he notified his Prior of his change of address, he briefly referred to the fact that he now got more fresh air and could once again speak to people. As for the fresh air, that often had unpleasant associations which he did not mention.

The first evening, as they lined up for a roll-call at 6 p.m., No. 58, as Titus Brandsma had become, stood with the rest and, like them, he was entirely bald. His hair, like theirs, had been shaven off to avoid the bother of de-lousing it. After the roll-call, the newcomers had to perform drill exercises. Their limbs were stiff with cold.

As they went inside, Father Aalders followed Brandsma into Block 11. He found him inside sitting on a bench at the large table, breaking his small portion of bread into even smaller bits. He managed to find a place next to Titus and suggested they should walk up and down a little to give themselves some privacy. Then, this new friend told Titus to hide the remainder of his bread as there were many who would be only too anxious to steal it. Unfortunately, the supervisor, who must have been suspicious of their movements, had followed them and stood listening. When he overheard this, he dashed forward and caught hold of them. Titus did his best to calm the fury of the man down.

The nights that followed weren't as long as in Scheveningen and were welcome after a hard day's work. The next morning was still very cold. No. 58 was made to join a group that had to shovel snow.

Two weeks before Titus's arrival, when the cold had become extremely severe, all dysentery patients had been moved to Block IV. For several hours they had been left on their mattresses outside the building and one of them had died. Another of them, the well-known Protestant minister, D. A. Van den Bosch, had become seriously ill and the news now went around that he was nearing his end. The camp, on Titus's first real working day, had become a silent place of gloom.

That evening the roll-call parade was extremely tiring and it was an hour before they could go to their barracks. Hardly had ten minutes gone by when they were recalled for another session of drill exercises. One of the prisoners' diaries records that when at last they could retire they had hardly time left to eat.[81] It went on like this for several days. On the 20th March, the news went through the camp that the Protestant minister, Van den Bosch, had died.

During one of the first days Titus was taken off snow-shovelling and put in a group that had to cut wood. In the woods that surrounded the camp the Nazis wanted a rifle range made. With axes and spades, saws and pickaxes, the group worked from eight in the morning until six in the evening, with one hour's midday break. Titus's hand must have trembled with exhaustion as he wrote his first note to Nijmegen: 'Don't worry, all is well.' That was all the news he gave.

In a short time even strong men lost twenty pounds. The death-rate was high, estimated at a quarter of the population a year. On Titus's first Sunday, 'Laetare Sunday', as ironically it was, Spring had begun to show itself with sudden unexpected generosity. To the fatigued and suffering community it seemed almost like a miracle.

Now, more than ever before, Titus must have wished that he could have inherited more of his ancestors' physical strength. Apart from the skating he had so much enjoyed in his child-hood, the fifteen-minute exercise at Scheveningen was probably the only physical exertion his slender body had ever undergone. In a letter which he was later to send from Kleve in Germany, Titus said it was 'providential' that during his period at Amersfoort he had been 'more or less ill' for five weeks. Fogtelo, who had been with Titus at Scheveningen, had also been transported to Amersfoort. He had noticed pretty soon that No. 58 could not cope with the hard work in the woods. After these first strenuous days, Fogtelo, with his con-nections in the camp, managed to get Titus out of it. It was none too soon, for shortly before his departure from Scheveningen,

Titus had been slightly affected by dysentery. His initiation into Amersfoort had done nothing to relieve his condition. It was decided to move him to Block IV for observation. The epidemic of dysentery which had broken out in the camp towards the end of February had already struck down about seventy-five victims.

The dysentery victims stayed in bunks which were placed above each other, in conditions of unbearable indignity. The stench was revolting and the nights especially were almost unendurable. Hardly anyone could remain in bed for longer than a couple of hours. Between the bunks were iron pails, covered by a piece of wood. Spasmodic pains accompanied every journey to them and these were repeated sometimes as often as five or six times a night. At first Titus' condition was better than some for, however rebellious his stomach, he didn't suffer from the constant high temperature which assailed many of his fellow sufferers.

The dysentery patients were not the only occupants of Block IV. Next to their quarters was a group of young Russian prisoners. They had been taken on frequent journeys for propaganda purposes. But once this was over, they were left to die, one after the other, of starvation and malnutrition. The dysentery patients always knew when one of them died for that evening the others sang on and on, their long lamentations seeping through the partitions and filling the whole building with sadness. By the beginning of April there were only a few of them left. They did not remain there long. After a few days they were put into cars which shortly afterwards returned empty except for a few excited SS guards. Nothing was said. There was no need. There was just more room in the camp.[82]

Before the dysentery bout was entirely over, Titus had left Block IV. On the Monday of Holy Week he returned to Block II as a convalescent. This meant greater freedom of movement. Later, he seems to have been given a light job but there is no certainty about this and it is open to doubt. All that is known is that on the 20th April he was seen waiting for a medical examination.

It was Hitler's birthday. To celebrate it, a group of Amsterdammer hostages were given their freedom. When they left, Titus gave one of them a message to Father Schiphorst of St Boniface's Church at Amsterdam with whom he had spent his last free evening. In it he mentioned the stomach pains he had been having. There was no question of a special diet to help him over this; only in his last week at Amersfoort was he allowed a kind of porridge instead of the normal menu of some soup together with the daily ration of bread and an occasional extra item of food, which had to keep body and soul together. There was also the permitted allowance of butter or margarine and a daily ration of coffee but the only merit of it was that it was warm. Some even added salt to it in a vain effort to improve it.

All the time Titus was in Amersfoort he wore a red triangle on his soldier's jacket which classified him as a political prisoner. Every group was distinguished by an insignia of this sort. The Jehovah Witnesses kept much to themselves. They read their smuggled Bibles and got themselves a bad name with the Nazis. They were distinctly marked by a violet insignia. The Jews were, of course, marked by the Star of David. When, after the war, some of them returned home, Rabbi J. Soetendorp was amazed to hear the name of Titus Brandsma constantly mentioned in their stories and recollections.

Fifteen days after Titus's arrival, a so-called court of law was established in the camp that was to decide the fate of the imprisoned members of the resistance organization. The whole of Holland was informed of the approaching process in the National Press and held its breath while it awaited the outcome. The inmates of the camp, well aware of the forthcoming trial, were living in a state of stress and strain as they lay between the fences and the fire-arms of the S.S. men, as isolated as if they were on an island.

For himself, Titus did not tremble but he became extremely concerned for others and went round the camp giving whatever spiritual comfort he could. He was referred to as 'the kindest man in the camp' and his busiest hours were those when, officially, he and the other prisoners were at leisure. It was at this time, after the evening roll-call parade and when they had eaten their ration of food, that they were more or less free until nine o'clock when the night formally began.

Unsurprisingly these hours of official leisure were often the hours of greatest sadness, and, during them, Titus's powers to comfort and sustain were taxed to their limit. As it was risky to call a priest 'Father', for the strictest prohibition was in force towards any form of spiritual care, many simply called him Titus. The young ones liked to call him 'Uncle Titus' and went to him constantly for courage and confidence. He suffered it all with a light and humourous grace.

One day twelve Jews arrived in the camp, one of whom was extremely upset. As soon as he found a suitable moment, one of the prisoners begged Titus to talk to the man. One of the bystanders later recalled how wonderfully Titus set about it. He put his hand on the Jew's shoulder and said: 'But, look old chap, if that is all you are worried about, having to put up with a little less food . . .' and he went on in the same vein teasing him gently until he was calmed and restored.

Without propaganda or preaching, but with a simple gesture and the charm of his personality, Titus Brandsma drew people out of their despair. He knew the difficult art of communication and this was his secret. He had done the same in Block IV with the dysentery patients. He had talked with them, prayed with them, tucked them in, shivering, into their bunks and warmed stones on the stove to put near their cold feet. A teacher from Oldenzaal, who had known Titus in former days, watched this unending manifestation of goodness with emotion. The same pattern repeated itself when Titus was a convalescent patient in Block II.

In a bunk opposite Titus was John Dons, one of the prisoners whom the so-called court would soon condemn to be executed. It is to John Dons that we owe the moving portrait of Titus Brandsma as 'prisoner No. 58'. A Baptist teacher by the name of Bleeker, with whom Titus talked in Frisian and revived other pleasant memories, later smuggled it out of the camp. It is a portrait of sadness: the shaven head, the soldier's uniform with the fountain pen and chain of his watch visible, the bony hand resting on the wooden table at which he was sitting. But Dons had seen much more, and this is in the portrait too. For around his mouth and his eyes lie a sure resignation and a deep inner peace, and more than in any earlier photographs his goodness is apparent.

Titus hadn't been long in the camp before everyone knew him and who he was, even the Nazis. He was to be seen in the company of the greatest possible variety of people with a jovial smile and a kind-hearted word for everyone. The young especially were devoted to him. One even volunteered to toast his bread.

One morning when he woke up, Titus's stomach was too upset to allow him to move and he failed to appear at the roll-call parade. By accident his name had not been listed among the patients. A raw voice asked who it was that was missing. Someone answered that it was Brandsma.

The apathy of the silent prisoners was suddenly broken. A whisper ran down the lines: 'Father Brandsma, Titus Brandsma, Uncle Titus is ill.' It was a strange moment of emotion roused by the name of a man whom everyone knew. One of those present, a young Dutch student, has never forgotten the quick murmur of Titus's name that went through the ranks of all those who loved him.

Titus did have one form of spiritual comfort for himself. Although he was unable to give or receive Communion, he no longer needed to say his rosary on his fingers. Before he left Scheveningen he had been given one through the intermediary of no less a person than a Protestant minister. It had been a gesture of understanding which he deeply appreciated. Somehow he had managed to hold on to it during, and since, his arrival in the camp.

Every morning when the bell rang at six o'clock, Titus, unless he was rendered immobile by dysentery, dressed and washed and could then be seen walking up and down, up and down. However cold it might be, those moments were for God and no one could take them from him or persuade him to spare himself a little.

What is surprising is that he still had his *Imitation of Christ* with him. He also had his book *Jesus* by Verschaeve which he had kept from Scheveningen. He constantly spoke to others about the '*Imitation*' and the pages of Verschaeve's book circulated among them as freely as circumstances permitted, except for those pages on which he had written his biography of St Teresa.

Perhaps Siegmund, a teacher of the lyceum at Oldenzaal, expressed better than anyone else what Father Brandsma meant to that polyglot community: 'He gave us a supernatural insight into our imprisonment,' he said and, on reading these words, one recalls Brandsma's spiritual points to the journalists. There, as here, and indeed during all the late stages of his final journey, he was concerned with the process of becoming a real Christian and with helping others to do the same.

Shortly before Titus's arrival at Amersfoort the Protestant minister, Van den Bosch, had been betrayed for the spiritual help he had been giving. Since then a public notice had been put up stating that it was utterly forbidden to use any biblical texts even in letters. It may be recalled that Van den Bosch's death which occurred during Titus' first days at Amersfoort as the result of dysentery, formed one of his first impressions of camp life. Priests and ministers realized that any attempt to organize some form of religious meeting entailed the danger of betrayal and a treatment by the Nazis which might break one for life.

Dr C. P. Gunning, Rector of a college in Amsterdam, had managed to visit the Protestant minister during his last days. He wanted to continue the work of this courageous man. 'No,' said the dying minister, 'it is no longer possible. Even the supervisor shall have to pay for it in the future.'

Since then, meetings were circumspect and only took place in the barracks in small groups. Usually on Sundays, after the hour for douching, which was the most unguarded and relaxed moment, the prisoners sat round in groups of five to ten, always on the alert for an alarm, with Titus among them. Sitting on the top bunk he improvised a spiritual exercise while holding a small missal in his hand.

A student from the University of Delft later recalled: 'It is now two years ago, but I can't read or hear the story of the disciples of Emmaus, without remembering the morning that Father Titus spoke to us about those men. I can hear him now explaining how their "stay with us, Lord" applied to us too, and how he prayed that Christ would stay with us in the camp of Amersfoort.'

Towards the end of his Sunday service, there followed a moving ritual, a kind of spiritual Communion, in which Titus Brandsma looked at each member of his audience in turn and said to them individually the liturgical words: 'May the Body of our Lord Jesus Christ preserve your soul unto eternal life.'

In spite of the fact that they were without the Eucharistic Presence, we know that Titus did not fail to convince his friends that the Lord was there among them:

'Where two or three are gathered together in My Name,' the Lord had said, 'There am I in their midst,' and with a telling gesture of his hand he conveyed the fact to them.

Holy Week began on the 29th March, 1942. Titus, availing himself of his qualified liberty as a convalescent, moved continually from one person to the other. He meditated with them on the Passion of the Lord. Once he was so deeply moved, apparently struck by the parallel between the lives of some of them and the Passion, that tears ran down his face.[83]

In the evening as well as in the morning they came for his blessing. One of them put it rather strongly when he said that they 'fought' for the opportunity. Titus gave it, of course, in the manner adopted by every imprisoned priest. He shook hands and, without any words, traced the sign of the cross upon it with his thumb. It left a consoling impression.

He often spoke about the Mother of God and tried to commemorate the Saint of the day. Once he was asked by the Protestant minister, Versteegh, one of the great men in the resistance movement, to tell a few non-Catholics about Theresa Neumann, the visionary of Konnersreuth. Seated at one of the tables, Titus spoke of the stories about her that had gone around the world and explained what he had seen for himself and thought of it all. Titus had seen the marks of the stigmata and had spoken to her a few years earlier. He took a cautious and sober view and suggested that a natural explanation might

be given, and that, in any case, it added nothing to one's
faith. One should never exaggerate the importance of mystical
phenomena, he pointed out, for, even when they come from
God, they do not add to His revelation but serve to help us to
steep ourselves more fully into the revelation He made to His
Church.

As Titus was a so-called 'convalescent' he was allowed to
walk about which gave him the chance to hear a good many
confessions inconspicuously. It is known that once he reconciled
people from different barracks. In Amersfoort, even some of
the guards came under his spell. He spoke to them, and asked
things of them, with such simplicity that it seemed to disarm
them. As a result, he was allowed to cross a couple of times a
day from the barracks to the 'hospital' quarters. He would
barely reach the bed of one he knew when, from all sides,
people called out to him. He went to Catholic and non-Catholic
alike.

Among the hospital patients were some Frisian gypsies and,
although their fellow prisoners took little notice of them, Titus
appeared as much at ease with them as with all the rest. When
the prisoners' conversation touched upon Karl Berg and the
other guards, he used to say: 'Just pray for these people.'

'Yes, but that is difficult,' someone said, to which Titus
replied in a matter-of-fact way: 'Well, you don't need to pray
for them all day long. God is quite pleased with one single
prayer.'

When it became known to the prisoners that Father Brandsma
had composed a poem while in Scheveningen, he used frequently
to be asked for copies of it and was quite happy to write it out
for whomever asked for it. He was once asked to recite it.
Calmly he went through the verses while his audience listened
silently, rumpling their soldiers' caps.[84] No one needed to feel
embarrassed for Titus himself was not. He completely lacked
self-consciousness and everything he did was done with genuine
lack of pretension.

While he was in the camp at Amersfoort, Titus struck up a
friendship with a young Protestant minister by the name of
Kapteyn. Together they were to travel the way of the Cross.

They often prayed together and another Protestant, Dr Gunning, who sometimes joined them declared that he 'felt himself very close to Titus in living the *Una Sancta.*' For Titus, now as in Nijmegen, made no distinction between Protestants and Catholics.

To while away the time, the Amsterdammer hostages occupied themselves with thinking out amusing slogans for the three letters P.D.A. which stared them in the face from the walls of the camp. These initials stood for *Polizeiliches Durchgangslager Amersfoort* or, in English, Transitory Camp of the Police at Amersfoort. Walking along the parade ground where the roll-call took place, Titus thought of a meaning which was perhaps the most profound of all. *Probamur dum amamur* ('We are being tried because we are being loved') with the variation: *Probemur dum amemur* ('let us be tried as long as we may be loved'). In these words Titus Brandsma had summed up the mysticism of human suffering.

On Good Friday, the 3rd April, Titus was to speak about this mystery of suffering. It may seem a sign of Providence that he was called upon to address a large audience of fellow prisoners about a subject so real everywhere in Europe. But nowhere more real than in Dachau where hatred culminated in an incredible way on Good Friday, possibly at the very hour when Titus Brandsma was speaking in the concentration camp at Amersfoort. A priest was actually crowned with thorns in Dachau; a Jew had to narrate the Passion, and many other priests had to sing: *O Haupt voll Blut und Wunden* ('O Sacred Head ill used').

What happened that last Good Friday in the life of Titus Brandsma had a prelude. In Block III, where part of the Amsterdammer intelligentsia lived together, a suggestion had been put forward on how to overcome the endless conversations about food which had become an obsession with the prisoners.

The atmosphere had become unbearably heavy since that fatal day in March, when religious subjects had been officially banned, because almost every day someone died. But now, Dr Gunning put forward the suggestion that Titus should speak in his barracks about a subject within his own field of studies: the history of mysticism. As many as possible were to be invited to this talk which, being historical, would not come under the ban. But, needless to say, the opportunity for a more spiritual interpretation would be great.

During that week the atmosphere had been rendered unendurable in the camp. The violence of the guards increased daily. On the Wednesday, one of the prisoners was kicked so inhumanely during the roll-call that he died before them on the parade ground. The special court that was to try the members of the resistance group had arrived and begun their sessions. They behaved with such exaggeration, and in such a ludicrous way, that it might have been funny had the prisoners not realized that something unusually serious was about to take place. By the morning of Good Friday the last group had been questioned by the court of officials. In the afternoon they would inspect the camp.

They arrived in polished boots and high caps for the inspection just as Titus was going to speak on a historical theme. It gave him the chance he needed. To his friend Van Mierlo, a director of an electricity company, who was still in the 'hospital' and therefore unable to be present, he could not remain silent about it. He would start, he explained, with a genuine piece of history about the place held by Geert Groote in Dutch literature. 'Then I can still say what I want.'

That same morning Titus had hurriedly written down on a piece of paper the points he was to raise. That piece of paper has been preserved and it is known that he held it in his hands when, at about 7 p.m., he began to speak. He was introduced by Dr Gunning and, during his lecture, stood on a box placed between two rows of bunks.

Sitting around the tables of the bunks were the guests from Block III with those from his own barracks packed between. Altogether an audience of well over a hundred inmates consisting of professors, priests, Protestant ministers, lawyers and journalists as well as those with far less academic background were present. All of them were in shabby soldiers' uniforms, suffering and half starved. The speaker leaned with his elbows on one of the bunks: an emaciated, small figure with vivacious eyes behind the thick glasses.

What was it that left such a deep impression on all those who survived to record the occasion? Everyone, agnostics and Christians alike, agreed that Brandsma's lecture was by far the most soul-stirring ever heard during their captivity, while those among them, given to expressing their judgement with greater reserve, ranked it among the best. Perhaps a priest who was present put his finger on it when he said that Titus seemed to speak to them then with his innermost soul. Colonel Fogtelo added that, that evening, he suddenly became aware for the first time since he had been in Amersfoort that somebody was speaking 'as if he was living in a free world.'

Titus's lecture dealt with the 'entirely diverse aspects' of mysticism as seen from a historical point of view. The Trinitarian mysticism had preceded Geert Groote of the *Devotio Moderna* to be crossed again with Ruusbroec by the Bernardine mysticism of espousal. The three ways of mystical practice were subsequently dealt with. Having set the stage in order to establish more precisely the exact place occupied by Geert Groote who owed much to the school of Ruusbroec, he had descended the 'steps of mysticism' and transferred the centre of gravity to the *via purgativa* and the *via illuminativa*. Geert Groote did not ascend; he did not count himself worthy but 'looked up to God coming down to us, God with us'. With that Titus had reached the leitmotiv of the spirit of the 'Imitation'. He was then able to introduce 'the passion of Jesus, the first object of our contemplation'.

The points on his piece of paper had served to pave the way. From then on, he seemed to have broken away from his notes and began to speak impromptu, saying things which touched the hearts. Gradually, imperceptibly, his lecture had become a meditation on the Lord's Passion of which his heart was so full.

When Titus finished no one spoke. Then a fellow don, who, with his elbows on the table, had listened and who now sought to break the silence with a flippant, murmured comment, said: 'I'm still glad that I am a Calvinist.' He shifted in his seat.

But most of the audience failed to hear the attempt to lighten the atmosphere.

'Quietly we went back to our places,' one of the audience recalled. 'Struck by God's spirit, no one said a word.'

For several days Titus appeared extremely tired. The effort had taken nearly all his strength, in addition to which, each day since he had been besieged by prisoners who wished to confess their sins and receive absolution. Their enthusiasm for his talk had been so great that they begged him to speak again. But it was obvious that he could not, or rather that he should not, for he was completely exhausted.

Unwisely, perhaps, Titus capitulated in response to their second invitation. It was either on Easter Sunday, or the day after, that Titus spoke to them about Father Brugman, one of the great men of the *Devotio Moderna*. Sadly his talk was a failure; the words came to him with great difficulty. Afterwards he was no longer capable of an academic dispute with one of the prisoners.

When he went back to his barracks with the humiliation of the past hour upon him, he took comfort perhaps from the fact that it was Easter and the memory of the bells which they all had heard in the camp that morning may have solaced him with a sense of peace and joy. Certainly he did not allude to his debâcle or waste time on regretting it. He had not enough vanity for that.

Easter Week was, in fact, a sombre one. On Tuesday the prisoners were made to decorate the S.S. canteen outside the gate with wood which was normally used for the camp fires. They framed portraits of Hitler, Himmler and Goering and, inevitably, constructed a swastika.

The following day the court sessions that had been going on all the time were to be brought to a close in the canteen. They ended with a long list of names of those who were to be executed for their part in the resistance organization. All of them had been placed under especially strict surveillance in Block IV.

Before the guards surrounded the barracks, several men made a final determined effort to speak to their friends inside. Titus was among them to give his sympathy and encouragement to those who were to go before him. He referred indirectly to it in his letter from Kleve to the Prior at Nijmegen when he asked him to let the family of an officer know how well-prepared the man had faced his death. He carefully indicated the officer's name by using a Latin word that would suggest it to anyone familiar with the language. It was, in fact, the greatest consolation to this man's relatives, for he had strayed far from his early principles and there was no other indication that he had ever returned to them.

In addition to the internal tension and misery within the camp during this unforgettable Easter, there were air raids during the night from Friday to Saturday which shook the bunks in which they were trying to rest.

Saturday began with glorious weather. From 1.30 p.m. to 3.30 p.m. the entire camp stood on the parade ground. When those two hours had passed, the seventy condemned men from Block IV, guarded by a couple of hundred soldiers, came out to face the other prisoners. For almost an hour they stood opposite each other, closely guarded by inscrutable S.S. men. If the Nazis hoped, by this means, to inculcate fear into those that had escaped the list, they made a psychological mistake, for the silence and stoicism of the convicted men impressed those that faced them in quite a different way.

Among them were some who stood with folded hands that deliberately pointed heavenwards. The effort to degrade them had failed and little remained but to allow the familiar trucks to drive through the gates and take them away. On the 3rd May, they were executed at Sachsenhausen-Oranienburg.

The day following the big parade, the rumour went around that the three prominent spiritual leaders, Brandsma, Höppener (Catholics), and Kapteyn (Protestant), had been put on the penalty list. Witnesses recall the fear that seized the prisoners and the prayer that went up all over in the camp, for everyone realized that Titus's chances of survival would be slim. The impression, however, that Titus's talk on Good Friday had made had not been lost on the Nazis.

His fellow prisoners thought of means to save him. A medical declaration, apparently followed by a short stay in the 'hospital' seemed, providentially, to have saved him so far. Titus knew, or had soon realized, that he was destined for Germany. 'I shall try to bear it,' was his only comment.

Dr Ronge, a Lutheran, who knew him then was of the opinion that such a man had to be 'very strong' and 'in ordinary life far above average'.

A talented son of the Mayor of Tilburg, who was moved from one camp to another over a period of three and a half years and who had met many distinguished men in the process under the most appalling circumstances, remembered Father Brandsma clearly from the seven weeks the latter spent in Amersfoort. When he tried, later, to compare him with the others, he had no doubt 'that Titus towered above them'. His judgement is of particular interest because he stresses the fact that Titus must not be thought of as having been stolid or impassive, insensitive or disinterested in his fate. 'He tried not to show it, but at times he was deeply saddened. Not because of self-pity but because of the knowledge, constantly before him, that men could do such things to one another. He never allowed his mental suffering to diminish his humour. He merely became quieter, more compassionate. Even for the bad element amongst the prisoners he had always kind and gentle words.'

The same witness goes on to say that the remarkable thing about Titus was the fact that all the prisoners with whom he came in contact remembered him so well in contrast to so many others they had long forgotten. He was struck by the goodness that emanated from him, as if suffering had refined him down to the real man within. Among his notes (as if to prevent any misunderstanding) one finds the words: 'He made me feel I had met a saint.'

The fact that Titus had experienced 'difficult hours' had not escaped the attention of his fellow priest, Father Hoppener. 'Only in very intimate conversations did his sadness reveal itself, and always in complete surrender to God.'

PART FOUR

The Road to Dachau

Chapter Twelve

SCHEVENINGEN AGAIN (CELL 623)

The last time the outside world had heard from Titus was when his letter of the 1st April reached the Priory at Nijmegen. It had ended: 'We will always remember each other.'

Since then, the message from the freed Amsterdammers had finally reached the parish priest of St Boniface's Church, who was only too aware that absolute secrecy was necessary. He had, therefore, passed on the contents of the message to the Archbishop, but not to the Community at Nijmegen.

Nothing more was heard until, on the 6th May, the telephone suddenly rang at the Priory at Nijmegen. The Prior, who was at home, lifted up the receiver and was amazed to hear Titus's voice. He couldn't believe it, and when he was forced to do so he realized with alarm the nature of the call.

Titus was in fact telephoning from Hardegen's room in The Hague. He had only been allowed to ring up in order to tell his Superior that, in a few days' time, he would be on his way to Dachau.

Together with a small group of other prisoners, among whom was Kapteyn, the Protestant minister, he had left Amersfoort on the 28th April. He had been given a very brief warning of his departure, but he had still managed to say good-bye to some of the men in the camp.

He was told to get out of his soldier's uniform and, once again, he found himself dressed in his black clerical suit, which he could hardly have expected ever to see again. Just as he was about to leave the camp, a fellow priest saw him and waved. Secretly, from a distance, Titus gave him his last blessing. Titus had been told that he would be kept under strict arrest as he was considered a dangerous man.

After he had left Amersfoort the rumour went around the camp that he had been given the chance of freedom provided he would sign some declaration. It is impossible, now, to substantiate this. It was, in any case, too vague a rumour to pay much attention to it. But one thing is quite certain: that he would certainly not have taken the opportunity if it had been offered him. In intimate conversation with fellow prisoners he had already faced the academic possibility and stressed, more than once, that, in the event, he would always categorically refuse to sign.[85]

It was late in the evening when he returned to the Oranje Hotel, the prison in Scheveningen. But he was not to find there the *beata solitudo* of the previous occasion, for during the short period he was to spend there, on this second visit, he was to share a small cell with two others.

Almost immediately after his arrival, the door of cell 623 was thrown open and he was urged inside. He could hardly see in the dark and neither could the two other occupants of the cell although they strained their eyes to see who had come to join them, and tried to make contact with him. They were two young men who were quick to realize that the newcomer was a frail, elderly man, and they immediately offered him the only bed available in their cell while they were content to sleep on a mattress on the floor. When they could see him better, they saw that he was 'terribly thin' and appeared to be 'very weak'.

One of the other prisoners in Scheveningen, who had been given certain prison duties and was entitled to move about the corridors while he did them, had known Titus as a boy.[86] He was delighted to see him, and used all his powers of persuasion to obtain a rickety arm-chair for him from the guards. He succeeded, but it wasn't easy. For Kirzig, one of the guards, was a rough, coarse man who had a particular dislike of Catholics and a large vocabulary of obscene words which he enjoyed using in their presence.

Yet, one day Kirzig remarked to the 'passage boy' that he wouldn't like to be in the front line opposite that man Brandsma: 'He's the sort of man who starts praying until a ruddy cross appears in the sky and wins the battles for him.'

A string of obscenities followed, but the 'passage boy' noticed all the same that Kirzig spent a lot of time spying on Titus through the spy-hole in the cell door. Finally his curiosity became too much for him and a remarkable thing happened. He took Titus out of his cell along the passage to the guardroom and kept him there talking far into the night.

Kirzig never spoke about this to the 'passage boy' until long after Titus's departure, when he said to him: 'That man was a saint.'

On his arrival at Scheveningen the guard must have taken his breviary and rosary away from Titus. Kirzig and the 'passage boy' succeeded in getting them out of the prison storeroom and returned them both to their legitimate owner.

Titus asked his Protestant companions in the cell whether it would disturb them if he prayed on his knees. No, that was quite all right, they replied, and accepted it with total lack of embarrassment. From then onwards they often saw him on his knees in prayer for long periods at a time.

He was very fortunate in having as his companions two young men who both believed in God. They talked to each other happily and at ease, and both were interested in discovering what a Carmelite was. The two Sundays they were together, they joined him in meditation and prayer.

Two days before Titus's departure was the Feast of Ascension. On that day, they had listened to him with great interest when he spoke about the gifts of the Holy Spirit. 'Those were great moments in our life,' one of them said later.[87]

After the evening meal the two friends relaxed and played cards while Titus prayed.

Several times he was taken to the Headquarters of the Polizei in The Hague. Once he stayed there the whole day. He had been fetched at nine in the morning and returned at seven in the evening. This was probably on the 6th May, the day on which the voice on the telephone at the Carmel at Nijmegen announced that Professor Brandsma was going to speak to them. He would be on the line immediately.

Titus had then told the Prior that he was telephoning from

the bureau of the Sicherheitspolizei in The Hague. He explained that he had been interrogated again and, as a result,
they had decided to send him to Dachau where he would
remain until the end of the war. He was to leave the next
Saturday and had been permitted to telephone as he needed
a few things with him such as his underwear.

When the Prior asked how things were with him, Titus
replied, 'All right,' and sent his affectionate greetings to
everyone. 'I can't say more,' he added, and the Prior, understanding, tried to say something quickly about the many
prayers that were being said on his behalf. But there was no
reply. The line had been cut.[88]

A report of the interrogation, dated the 6th May, 1942,
went to the Reichssicherheitshauptamt in Berlin, but only the
content of the accompanying letter is known.[89] Later, from
the transitory prison at Kleve, Titus revealed the fact that he
had been questioned about certain letters, no doubt the ones
they had laid their hands on when they had originally arrested
him at Carmel.

From the German report *Meldungen aus den Niederlanden*
referred to earlier, one thing is quite clear: nothing could have
occurred, since his original arrest, which gave the Nazis any
fresh light on the case of Titus Brandsma.

On his return that evening, his cell companions noticed that
Titus had been given a supply of paper and ink. He told them
the reason and settled down to his task of re-writing his
objections against National Socialism.

As we have said before, there is every reason to believe that
this task imposed on him for the second time concerned the
same questions which Hardegen had ordered him to write
about four months ago in January. One copy is thought to be
the original January draft Titus had kept himself (see page
116).

He was to remain in Scheveningen a few more days, plenty
of time, therefore, to contemplate the future that lay in store.
He confided to the 'passage boy' that he still had a great deal
to do during his life, but he was not afraid to die. The young
man got the impression that Hardegen had tried to win Titus

to the Nazi point of view and was angry at his failure to do so.

Two members of the Sicherheits Dienst, Woysky and Horac, tried to find out from one of Titus's cell companions whether he had ever talked to them about his views. They added that he had been foolish for, by making a small retraction, he could have walked out a free man. But Titus had placed himself in God's hands. He was prepared to do all he reasonably could to stay alive but no more if it involved any betrayal of principles.

For his companions those were eighteen pleasant days lit up by Titus's kindness and lightness of touch. To meet him accidentally in the corridors was to be consoled or welcomed with warmth. To live with him in the same cell was to be, and to feel, near a fountain of grace. He thought of others constantly, even refusing to allow them to make his bed once his strength returned, and he listened with genuine interest and concern to what they had to say. It was no wonder that they missed him when, before three weeks were over, he left them.

Chapter Thirteen

KLEVE

On Saturday, the 16th May, Titus crossed the Dutch-German border. How he travelled is not known for certain but it is probable that he passed through Nijmegen on his way. It had been a farewell gesture of affection on the part of the 'passage boy' to ensure that his shoes were repaired before he left. The soles had been completely worn out.

For Hardegen, Brandsma's case was now closed. It was soon to be finally sealed for Brandsma himself. Ignorant of this, the Prior visited Hardegen in an effort to discover what lay behind Titus's latest sentence.

Hardegen confirmed that Titus had telephoned the Prior from the very room he was now in, but would reveal nothing more. The case, he repeated, was now out of his hands and beyond his control.

The prison in Kleve was used by the Gestapo as well as by other more reputable authorities. The Gestapo had no official keys but were 'permitted' to speak to the prisoners they had brought there and, at their own discretion, take them away. There was, therefore, a continuous stream of coming and going. Kleve was a distribution centre, a transitory prison for men and women from the occupied countries. The duration of one's stay at Kleve depended upon whether there were enough prisoners from any one country to make a transport to the ultimate destination worthwhile.

Ludwig Deimel, who was later to become a doctor in theology, was, at that time, the curate in Kleve and acted as prison chaplain there. He has always maintained that the staff of the prison were, on the whole, against National Socialism. And that so was the prison director. Perhaps, as a result, the conditions in the prison at Kleve could be described as very good. There was only one man there who could legitimately be described as rough or cruel. It was unfortunate but it was with this man that Titus sometimes found himself.

As for the food, Deimel considered it qualitatively rather good. It was well cooked but whether there was enough of it he couldn't say for certain. But of one thing he was sure. It was possible to smoke quite a bit and this was a great comfort as the transitory prisoners had to stay all day in their cells apart from their morning and evening walk in the prison's garden. The moment he got to Kleve Titus was able to see the doctor.

As he entered the waiting room he suddenly recognized a friend from Amersfoort. 'We literally threw ourselves into each other's arms,' the friend wrote later. They were never to see each other again.

The doctor prescribed bread and porridge, but one of the odd results of his prescription was that Titus was no longer given the butter, fat, and meat to which he was entitled as part of the ordinary prison menu. Perhaps that is why he mentioned it in his letter home. But he did not mention another side to the story which a fellow prisoner has given us.

At the time that he received his special menu, Titus continued to turn up every day to collect the ordinary rations. He gave this illegally obtained portion to an Italian with whom he shared his cell. The man was always hungry and complained of his hunger the whole day long.[91]

The fact that Titus gave his ration to the Italian appears the more generous when one reads his comment in the letter just referred to: 'I seem to have developed a ravenous appetite for the first time in my life.'

But inevitably retribution occurred. One day the guard spotted Titus collecting the illegal portion of food and reviled him harshly in front of the rest. Perhaps this made him keep a special eye on Titus. Anyway, he watched him suspiciously and, shortly afterwards, again took action. On the inside of his cell door Titus had stuck up a cross made of paper. When the guard next inspected his cell he saw it and swore at him furiously.

On another occasion the guard, whose duty it was to super-vise the prisoners during their walk in the garden, called him out of the queue and made him return to his cell because he had noticed him whispering something to the prisoner in front.

What actually happened was that the man in front of Titus had looked around carefully a couple of times and, thinking himself unobserved, had at last asked, out of the corner of his mouth, 'Aren't you Professor Brandsma?'

It was his answer to this question that the guard intercepted. Later, the man in question spoke of the heart-warming words the Professor had addressed to him in that brief whispered comment.

It was fortunate that the prisoners in Kleve were not beaten by the guards, as they would have been in Amersfoort, or Titus would have been in serious trouble.

According to the reminiscences of Deimel, the prison chap-lain, although they are not corroborated by other evidence, Titus was re-united in his last days at Kleve with his friend from Amersfoort, Kapteyn, the Protestant minister. If so, nothing could have given him greater comfort, for in his company Titus felt he had found his greatest spiritual friend. The fact that they were actually put into the same cell, as Deimel's evidence suggests, is very consoling to those who loved Brandsma for they were united with each other. Kapteyn, too, died in Dachau in 1942.

Kapteyn was thirty-four years old and on the authority of Aukes, the author of the Dutch standard work on Brandsma, he occupies a rare place in the various memoirs published after the war. Later, a Belgian priest[92] was to see them together in Dachau and was deeply moved by their obvious and profound affection.

While he was at Kleve, Titus was once more allowed to go to Communion. The opportunity delighted him. It even encouraged him to ask Deimel if there was any chance at all of his being allowed to say Mass. The answer was finally in the negative. It was quite out of the question. But the very

first Sunday he was there Titus had been able to attend Mass
in the prison chapel, and again on Whit Sunday and Monday.
The organ had played and there were even flowers on the
altar. Here, too, Titus was allowed to keep his breviary and
rosary with him in his cell. He found himself among several
old prison friends at Kleve. He was becoming quite an 'old boy.'
Kleve, like Scheveningen, had its 'man in the corridor'. He
happened to be a fellow-Catholic from Utrecht by the name
of de Groot who often sought a chance to speak to Titus.
Usually when he did he found Titus in prayer. But Titus would
at once make the sign of the cross and willingly interrupt his
prayer for a few moments. He often spoke to De Groot about
God and the necessity of keeping in touch with Him. de Groot
later remarked to the Prior at Nijmegen that 'no interruption
was ever an inconvenience to him'.

Under the pretext of hearing his confession, Deimel, the
chaplain, was able to take Titus to the sacristy where he could
discuss with him certain intellectual matters that preoccupied
him. They talked together about the philosophical opinions of
Karl Jaspers and Deimel lent Titus some books for which the
latter was extremely grateful.

It was during these talks with the chaplain that Titus
discussed the idea of making an appeal to the authorities. He
drew up a detailed written report about his health and asked
to be placed under house arrest in a monastery in Germany.
In his letter home, dated the 25th May, he had written: 'I am
healthy again; my usual complaint (the urine infection) though
uncared for hardly troubles me. During these four months I
have experienced only a little disturbance and pain and that
only on three occasions. In the circumstances I am really doing
remarkably well.'

The request of the 12th June, however, tells a different story.
It must, of course, be borne in mind that it was a piece of
special pleading that was not intended for the eyes of friends
and relatives at home, and that in it Titus was making the
worst of things whereas generally he was trying to make the
best. Nevertheless a lot of what he says in this report has been
confirmed by fellow prisoners. He mentions long periods of

mental dullness which accompanied a near state of collapse, and frequent loss of memory which was sometimes serious, as well as a growing inability to sleep at night.

The picture fits in with what several fellow prisoners later reported about that time – that he often repeated himself as if he had forgotten what he had just said.

The request mentioned that, for several days he had tried to recall the name of the French philosopher Bergson, without success. Yet, philosophy was, in fact, the field in which he specialized. At times he seemed to hear the ringing of bells and, once or twice, when he had played draughts he kept on seeing the chequered board long afterwards, dazzling his inner vision. He felt deathly tired all day long and was forced to sit down after the least physical effort. The rough draft of the request was found in the brim of his hat when, after his death, all his possessions were sent back to Nijmegen.

Again, one must point out here that these last symptoms were not his general and permanent condition. They were written in the present tense and Titus was intent on putting his case as strongly as in conscience he could. The chaplain, and later others in Dachau, confirmed that he was in full possession of his spiritual faculties all the time. Deimel added that his appearance was 'very fine and spiritualized' and that his movements were quick.

The failure of his request did not perturb Titus in the least. 'Nothing shook the peace of his soul,' Deimel said.

On Titus's request, Deimel had taken over his formal appeal for house arrest and given it to someone who would personally deliver it to the Priory at Nijmegen whence the appeal could be addressed to Hardegen in The Hague.

The community at Nijmegen were in a slight quandary over this. They did not know what to do as Hardegen had already made it very clear to them that the case was closed when they had made a similar plea on the strength of an earlier letter from Titus shortly after his arrival in Kleve. Now that they had been asked to hand on Titus's formal and personally written request, might Hardegen not suspect a conspiracy?

After some hesitation and a great deal of discussion, however,

A portrait by John Dons, who was later executed, drawn in the
Amersfoort concentration camp

The concentration camp at Dachau

they decided that nothing worse could happen, and it was just possible that some good might come out of it. Accordingly they sent off the plea. At the same time, from Kleve, the chaplain had written to the Prior of the Carmel at Bamberg in Germany asking if he would be prepared to take Titus there if the opportunity arose.

But time was up. No replies had been received from either Hardegen or the Priory at Bamberg when Titus was put on the transport train which was to take him via Cologne to Dachau. He had been at Kleve for nearly a month.

The chaplain advised Titus to request a medical examination in Cologne, as the prison doctor at Kleve could not be trusted. Also Professor Steffes at Munster, who had lectured at Nijmegen University, directly appealed to Seyss-Inquart on behalf of Titus. Unknown to Titus a great deal of activity was, in fact, going on to try and achieve his liberty. It was still going on when his death cancelled everything.

By the time of Titus's departure from Kleve, he and Deimel had become fast friends and the chaplain had even managed occasionally to give Titus Holy Communion on weekdays. Deimel's mother, hearing him speak so highly about Professor Brandsma, prepared a little present for him now and then which was usually something comforting to eat.

Ten days before he was put aboard the transport train Titus had sent a letter to his brother Henry, the Franciscan, in Holland to congratulate him on his sixtieth birthday. Who would have thought, he said, that his brother would ever have to congratulate him on such an event from prison? He also gave Henry Brandsma a message from *Frisia Catholica* in which he asked the Frisians to build the Stations of the Cross at Dokkum from the ruins of pre-Reformation monasteries. He indicated in his letter where they could be found and who had promised him their support. He hoped that his brother would begin his new year with joy. 'I share in that joy,' he ended.

After the war, the chaplain of the Kleve prison received an enquiry form from the Vicar General of the Diocese of Munster in which Deimel was requested to inform his Superiors of any

German, or foreign, martyrs of Nazi National Socialism. Deimel replied that, among the thousands of prisoners he had attended, he had met two saints. In his report, however, he only mentions one – Titus Brandsma himself.

Chapter Fourteen

DACHAU

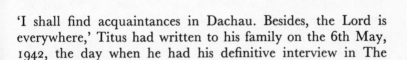

'I shall find acquaintances in Dachau. Besides, the Lord is everywhere,' Titus had written to his family on the 6th May, 1942, the day when he had his definitive interview in The Hague. He had expected to be sent there at once.

But Himmler and his accomplices had no dearth of victims. For a few weeks Titus had to wait in Kleve from where he wrote: 'I shall be long enough in Dachau. There is no point in being anxious to get there.'

But on Saturday, the 13th June the hour had come. He was chained and put on the transport train in the company of his friend Kapteyn.

Efforts to reconstruct the six days that it took them to reach Dachau have not been very successful. Only the general outline has been established.

Several Belgian priests were also transported on the same day from Brussels to Germany. We know that their train halted at Gladbach in Germany and awaited the arrival of another train. When this drew in a number of passengers were moved over into the train carrying the Belgians. Titus Brandsma and Kapteyn were among them.

They were pressed into a very small compartment where they joined four other prisoners, among whom was the Belgian Abbé Delcourt to whom we owe some of our information. They travelled in the cell-cars which crossed and re-crossed Europe during those years with their loads of prisoners destined for the concentration camps and gas chambers.

Unfortunately, though hardly surprisingly, Delcourt's account is not clear as regards the events of this journey. His impressions are clear but seem to have been confused with a later journey he made from Dachau. But about Titus himself his impressions were firm. 'I saw immediately what sort of man he was: somebody who moved at ease in a large spiritual domain.' Their rapport had been immediate and spontaneous: 'He joined us rather than led us and he made no attempt to display his knowledge.'

To kill the time, Titus had told them about a congress he had attended. He sought for points of contact with the others and spoke about people he had met. As he did so, Delcourt records, *Ses yeux voyaient le monde* ('his eyes saw the world').

How long did it take the train to cover the short distance to Cologne? It is difficult to be sure. For the area round Cologne had just undergone a tremendous bombardment. Less than two weeks previously it had been heavily bombed night after night. It was to be expected that the prisoners' transport would encounter considerable delay.

On Monday, the 15th June, two days after they had left Kleve, a German priest met Titus and his friend Kapteyn when they were led into the prison at Frankfurt. (He could not be absolutely certain about the date, but this is what he thought it was.) And, to the many new names and friends who accompanied Titus on his last journey, we must now add the name of this priest. He was Heinrich Rupieper. Rupieper had dedicated himself to youth work. After the 1933 Nazi take-over he had been left unmolested for just another two years. Then, accused of agitating from the pulpit against the new regime, he had been given a sentence of four years' imprisonment, but they had kept him a prisoner ever since. When he met Titus at Frankfurt, he had just come from Neuengamme. Rupieper had seen many camps but admitted unwillingly that Dachau was one of the worst, and he gave Titus a few useful hints about camp life.

The following day the prisoners appear to have journeyed further. Travelling with Titus, were Kapteyn, Abbé Delcourt, de Coninck, the well-known Belgian Jesuit, Heinrich Rupieper, and Redecke, a priest from the diocese of Aachen. With the exception of Kapteyn, the Protestant minister, all of them were priests. This may seem surprising but in fact a great many priests ended up in Dachau.

The camp office files show that a total of more than two hundred and six thousand prisoners were registered between 1933 and 1945. In addition, of course, many prisoners were taken to Dachau without being registered at all. The exact figures are unknown. According to Mgr Joh. Neuhäusler,[93] in 1942 there were two thousand, seven hundred and twenty ministers of religion in Dachau of whom eight hundred and fifty were Polish priests; a hundred and nine were Protestant ministers and there were thirty-two religious leaders of other denominations. On the other hand, P. van Gestel, S.J., states in the *Osservatore Romano* of the 21st April, 1947 that in 1942 there were one thousand, six hundred priests and ninety non-Catholic ministers.

In comparing the various sources of information, the total number of prisoners in 1942 is to be estimated at approximately twelve thousand. The German priests were kept together while priests from the other occupied countries stayed in Blocks 28 and 30.

Continuing their journey, they left Mainz behind, steamed into Bavaria and reached Nuremberg in the evening.

For a few days they were to find shelter in the Turnhalle, which was a vast gymnasium there. Someone who arrived there a week later described it as 'a great receptacle of European misery'. Every tribe and tongue were represented in the huge crowd which huddled together in a state of uncertainty and fear which defies description.

The first evening they arrived they were given nothing to eat. The following morning they received two slices of bread and some coffee. That was to be all for the day.

The atmosphere was stifling. Somewhere in a corner stood a single fountain for the hundreds of men to drink from. Here and there, at strategic points, stood already half-full barrels by way of lavatories. The stench grew steadily worse as two or three miserable days and nights passed.

They may have counted themselves fortunate when at last they were told to move on. Although the train was passing through some of the most beautiful landscape of Bavaria, they would have seen nothing of it.

It was five o'clock in the afternoon of the 19th June when the train with its load of prisoners pulled in at the station of Dachau. Once more they were handcuffed. Titus and his companions were part of a large group of prisoners, and all were stiff and exhausted from their journey and the conditions that had prevailed before it. Small transport cars stood on the platform waiting for them. When a prisoner didn't get in quickly enough, the S.S. men were ready to help with the butts of their rifles. Dachau is not far from Munich and lies, ironically enough, in the heart of Catholic Bavaria. Just a few miles outside Dachau lay the concentration camp with its large attendant S.S. camp.

As the transport cars drove the newcomers through the gates of the camp they could see above the gates, in crude iron lettering, the words: *Arbeit macht frei* ('Work makes free'). It was a wry comment on the truth – almost, in the circumstances, a joke. The Germans were keen on their jokes; indeed they prided themselves on them. A week later, in reply to the question about his occupation in more normal times, one Protestant minister had answered that he was a minister of Religion; the S.S. man had laughed: 'How fortunate,' he said, 'you are perfectly placed to celebrate the Ascension in a fortnight's time.' It is quite possible that Titus was treated to the same joke.

Rupieper noticed that Karl Kapp, one of the supervisors in the camp singled out Titus at once but it was not an attention that anyone could have sought or appreciated.

From the numbers they got, it is clear which of them were with Titus, who got No. 30492. Kapteyn, Delcourt, de Coninck, Rupieper and Redecke were all together. Under the sharp bright lights they were told to undress and undergo the humiliating ceremony of 'vermin control'. The bath-master enjoyed his sadistic prerogative of pushing the newcomers into a bath of biting fluid.

Dressed in blue-grey striped trousers and jackets (rather like pyjamas), wooden sandals, and a cap designed to make them

look and feel foolish, they were then herded to the entrance
barracks where they were to be instructed, now and later, with
endless precision in the niceties of marching and saluting
properly. They were also taught how to make their beds in
the appropriate prison manner. At this Titus was singularly
bad. Never very handy, he managed to get it wrong time and
time again, in spite of the fact that on every occasion he was
severely beaten.

He was not very good at marching either, even with the
encouragement given him by the instructor from Berlin who
enjoyed stepping on his heels so that the blood ran down the
back of his feet. On one occasion, in his anxiety to keep in
step, he lost his sandals. It was a moment the instructor had
been waiting for. On his bare feet, Professor Brandsma had to
march in quick tempo over the uneven stones while the
instructor struck him, and kept on striking him, in time with
his marching.

Then and later, Titus showed nothing of his feelings.
Rupieper advised him to launch a complaint. He knew that it
had sometimes helped, but Titus reacted in his own way. He
didn't think it was the moment for complaining: 'We are
going to pray for these men,' he said. And he did.

He prayed a lot of the time, even while they were standing
on the parade ground. In brief concealed chats, he tried to
console his neighbours. Rupieper fell completely under his
spell. After a few days in the train and barely two weeks in
the barracks, almost everyone near him knew enough about
Titus Brandsma to call him 'exceptional'.

Then the moment everyone dreaded arrived. The friends
were separated. Rupieper and, presumably, Redecke were
taken to Block 26, where the German priests stayed, while
Titus went to Block 28 where the Polish priests stayed. On each
side of the Lagerstrasse (the main camp road lined with poplar
trees that were planted by the first prisoners) stood fifteen
Wohnbaracken, so-called Blocks (the barracks in which the
prisoners were housed), two infirmaries, a canteen, and a
workshop barrack. Each *Wohnbaracke* was divided into four
Stuben (a living-room and dormitory unit). Two of these *Stuben*

had to share one wash-room and the lavatory. One *Stube* was to accommodate fifty-two prisoners, that is, two hundred and eight prisoners per barrack. Eventually the camp became so overcrowded that up to one thousand, six hundred prisoners had to live in one barrack.

Willy Bader, the reasonable Stubeälteste who managed to preserve some humanity in the most degrading circumstances, was to warn a Protestant minister about the two Polish barracks. It was a hell there, he told him; the S.S. men on duty in those barracks were devils who didn't allow their prisoners a minute's rest. They died like rats.

It is known that, by the end of the war, at least eight hundred and fifty Polish priests had died in Dachau, while according to the files of the International Tracing Service a total of at least thirty-one thousand, nine hundred and fifty-one died in the camp. Over and above that number a few thousand prisoners who had not been registered at all were killed by shooting.

A gas chamber, camouflaged as a shower room, which had been installed in Dachau upon orders of the S.S. Economic Administrative Main Office in Berlin was not used. The prisoners selected for 'gassing' were transported from Dachau to the Hartheim Castle near Linz in Austria, or to other camps. In Hartheim alone thirty-one thousand, six hundred and sixty-six prisoners were gassed between January 1942 and November 1944.

As the crematorium, constructed outside the prisoners' compound in 1940, proved to be too small, a larger one was built by the prisoners of 1942. The mortuary was permanently crammed with corpses.

A ditch, a live barbed-wire obstacle and a high wall, lit up at night, surrounded the camp. If a prisoner stepped onto the strip of grass, twenty-seven feet in front of the ditch, the S.S. men in the guard towers above shot him without warning.

On 12th July, Titus wrote his last letter. It was addressed to Oegeklooster, the place where he was born and where his sister lived in their old farmhouse. For the last time he wrote his comforting stereotyped comment: 'All is well with me.' It was followed by: 'One has to adjust oneself of course to new situations, which with God's help one manages here as well as elsewhere.' He ended up asking the family 'not to worry too much about me,' and signed himself, 'In Christ, your Anno.'

By this time he had been three weeks in Dachau, half of which time he had spent in Block 28. His day began at four o'clock in the morning when a siren sounded. The quicker he could get dressed the more time he had left for performing the crazy ceremony of the making of his bed. Then to the wash-room, where one ate what little food one had spared the previous evening, polished one's plate and cup before marching in military step to the roll-call ground. One didn't get much time there either but at least one could get one's breath back and stand still while the other prisoners were being counted. Those few moments, as they all knew, were the opportunity for a quickly whispered conversation or for private prayer.

It would be nearly five o'clock before the counting was done and they were dismissed to join their particular work com-mando. Here and there one spotted a friend and, if one were agile enough, could cross each other's way and say a quick word in passing.

Twenty-five minutes later Titus Brandsma was at work. At the quick march, he and his group of about one hundred had gone to the 'Liebhof' garden. On the way they had to sing typical German songs which they had been taught in the entrance barracks. There was nothing surprising about this, for the Germans loved singing while they marched.

The prisoners were accompanied by S.S. men and their dogs. The landscape was flat and monotonous, but sometimes on bright sunny days a wonderful view could be had towards the south of the mountains in the far distance. Many well-known painters have depicted the scenery there for the skies can be endlessly beautiful and so can the panorama. Perhaps once in a while, the view lifted Titus's heart and no doubt gave him a nostalgia for home and peace, not that one was given much time for nostalgia or lyrical feelings. The prisoners had to weed, dig the heavy soil, plant medicinal herbs such as basili-cum, a pepper substitute, and other green crops.

Their wooden sandals had been exchanged for shoes with

wooden soles and hard leather on top but it only took a few days before Titus' feet, already kicked and wounded, showed a number of big ulcerating wounds. The long marches to and from work became a torment which was sometimes unbearable, but at least in the 'Liebhof', which the prisoners had nick-named 'Friedhof', ('cemetery') they were allowed to take off their shoes and socks and to work barefoot.

They worked, ceaselessly bending over the ground, from 5.30 to 11.30 a.m. on a practically empty stomach, without rest and without even a drink of water. Then they were marched back to the camp and given half an hour to take some miserable soup with a little vegetable in it and one or two potatoes. They washed and polished their dishes and marched back to work again where they laboured until they were returned to the camp at seven in the evening.

On every journey, including their final return at night, they had to sing as well. Once they had arrived back at the camp they had to suffer the evening roll-call parade which could take as long as thirty minutes but sometimes lasted for an hour and even longer. After that they collected their rations which consisted of three and a half ounces of bread each, which had to do for the next morning as well. They also got a little butter and a couple of peeled potatoes.

Often, in fact very often, the much-hated ministers of God had to do an extra half-hour's exercise before being allowed to eat. They had to march again, do 'press-ups' off the ground, get up again, take their caps off, put them on again, get down again, and so on. And woe betide the man who couldn't keep up the tempo, or who wasn't in line with the others.

At last night came and they were able to retire around nine o'clock.

Often prisoners died on the 'Liebhof' but, whether dead or dying, every single man had to be dragged back to the roll-call parade, for the numbers had to be accounted for.

It did not take long before Father Titus had to be helped back by those near him. On the 'Liebhof' he was clearly an exhausted man. When the guards weren't near, his friends laid him flat on the ground for a few minutes to recover. During those moments they often prayed together aloud. Though Becker was the S.S. man in charge of Block 28, in 'Stube' 11, which was Room 111 of the barracks, Walther Thiel more or less reigned supreme. He was a brute who cruelly tormented Titus on many occasions. He was once seen beating Titus in the face with his bowl which opened up a wound which bled freely on Titus' already emaciated face.

A fellow prisoner, Father H. Kuyper, recalled that not only was Titus unable to cope with the physical conditions of the camp, but he lacked a certain knack of getting himself out of difficult situations. Again and again, when others got away with it, he was caught and punished. People who, in their own misery, watched him from nearby with love and concern, agreed with one another that he wasn't handy or agile on his feet. In the general turmoil he couldn't get out of the way of the guard quickly enough. He became that dreaded thing – the butt and target of a soldier's wit.

One day Titus had forgotten his glasses. He had left them in his 'Stube' but Walther Thiel stood in the open doorway. No one was ever allowed to go back.

Titus waited for the moment when Thiel would move away and crept inside. But, once inside, he stumbled and made a noise which caused Thiel to dash back.

'What does this mean, Brandsma?' he shouted.

'I had forgotten my glasses,' Titus replied and tried to go out. But before he reached the exit a terrific stroke with the stick had thrown him to the ground.

'That will teach you to forget them again,' yelled Thiel and struck him over and over again.

When he stopped, Titus took a long time to get up. When he at last did so, Tijhuis, a Dutch Carmelite brother who always tried to be near to Titus and help him, picked up his glasses and gave them back to him. But even this Carmelite colleague could not always be in the immediate vicinity. A person noticed an incident of this sort happening to another, but no one spoke about these things. It was neither expedient nor even always possible.

One morning the entrance doors to the barracks had been

painted and the prisoners were expected to enter by a different way. Exhausted from working and failing to notice the warning sign, Titus went in through the wrong door. In a fury, Thiel rushed up to him and hit him several times across the face with his fist.[94] 'If anyone was a martyr, then it was Titus,' remarked the eye-witness who wiped the blood away.

After the war, De Coninck, the Belgian Jesuit, wrote an article about the priests in Dachau. He mentioned only a few of his former companions by name for there were so many of his fellow sufferers, but Bishop Kozal of Poland and Titus Brandsma were clearly referred to. He said that Titus went to his death 'happy that he had been treated like the scourged Christ', though Titus himself would never have put it like this. Histrionics were not his line. But there is no doubt that his sense of inner peace, of joy almost, was so deep that he conveyed it to everyone around him.

It is extraordinary that during his short stay in Dachau, a matter of five weeks, Titus Brandsma should have left the profound impression he did. He was, after all, one of many who were suffering equal misery and degradation, where it was a terrible struggle merely to stay alive. But Dr Kentenich, who knew him for only two or three weeks, remarked in 1954 that 'his person and his words suggested such calm, such resignation and so much hope, that one does not easily forget it.'

He still remembered what Titus had told him: 'Jetzt soll ich halt leben was ich anderen früher gelehrt habe.' ('Now I will have to put into practice what I have previously taught others.')[95]

After the war, Urbanski, a Polish priest, wrote a book about Dachau which dealt almost exclusively with the martyrdom of his own compatriots. Yet he, too, felt compelled to mention Titus Brandsma. The fact that he himself was a Carmelite and that it was he who (together with the Prior of the monastery of Cracaow) had supported Titus on the way back from the 'Liebhof', probably played a part in his recollections. But the fact remains that the few days he had known Titus served to make a lasting impression. Long afterwards he could picture

Titus's kind and smiling face and even recall his words 'that touched the heart'. He still remembered those brief moments when Titus communicated with his Polish colleagues, 'so serene and accessible, so happy in the midst of danger that threatened everywhere'. Another Polish priest, Dr Boleslaw Wyszynski, was still in the so-called hospital of the camp when Titus arrived in Block 28. After a few days he was returned to the Polish barracks and observed how upset Titus felt whenever a fellow prisoner was inhumanely beaten.

'Father Brandsma was then already in pretty bad shape,' Wyszynski added, 'physically very emaciated and weak, but he communicated a great tranquillity of spirit.'

He, like others before him, used the phrase *gesammelt* to describe him. Unfortunately there is no exact English equivalent but, in the context, it means that Titus was in possession of himself, of his faculties and of his soul. The explanation, endorsed by so many eye-witnesses, was that he lived in uninterrupted union with God.

Without reserve he consoled, encouraged, heard confessions in the *Stube*, or wherever the chance presented itself, and encouraged others to keep in touch with God.

It seems unbelievable in the circumstances but the Eucharistic Presence of Christ was allowed in Dachau at least from the beginning of 1941.

In January 1941, an order was suddenly given to erect a small chapel in Block 26, the barracks occupied by the German priests. Was it part of a diplomatic game? We do not know, only that it was allowed and that Mass was said there daily. Soon the fact became known. In Blocks 28 and 30 it must have brought some consolation. No doubt Titus, like others among the foreign priests, turned his eyes sometimes towards the green-painted windows of that nearby Block where, in the very early hours of the morning, the mystery of the Redemption was re-enacted. Anyone who was caught listening in was severely punished, for the guards knew that a system of smuggling the consecrated Hosts had been established.

The ways in which the Hosts were actually carried to priests outside Block 26 was, of course, a kept secret. Too much was at stake for it ever to be revealed. But we do know that, once or twice at the evening meal, a Capuchin friar was able to hide the Host between the potatoes which he gave to Titus. Another prisoner in the Polish barracks had a standing agreement with a German priest in Block 26. Immediately after the morning roll-call, when everyone was struggling to get to his own particular work commando and crossing and re-crossing each other, he would try to meet the German and take the Host from him in passing. In the evening he could then hand it to Titus who would quickly conceal it in his spectacle case before returning to his barracks.

One evening there was a near panic. Titus had returned utterly exhausted from the 'Liebhof'. He got through the roll-call only to find that it was one of those occasions when the priests had to stay on for another spell of exercise. Still, Titus got through, although it was obvious that he could barely manage to eat, polish the bowl and wash. What they had all feared for some time was now going to happen.

On his return to Block 28, Thiel inspected him and was patently not satisfied. He beat and kicked Titus as if he had gone mad. He was watched by others in an agonizing silence. With his spectacle case still pressed under his arm, Titus had managed to crawl towards the doorstep of Block 28 where the Dutch friar, Raphael Tijhuis, helped him to get back into his bunk. There was no need to console Titus. He waited until Thiel was safely out of the way then, smiling, he said: 'I knew Whom I had with me!'

He then suggested that together they should say the *Adoro te* and, with a barely perceptible gesture, he blessed the friar with his peculiar ciborium.

The following morning Tijhuis learnt that Titus had spent a poor night as far as sleeping was concerned and that those sleepless hours had been spent in union with God. Nothing, moreover, would stop him from trying to bring the guards back to God and their humanity, in spite of all his fellow prisoners did to dissuade him. He talked to the guards and tried to make contact with them. When Tijhuis attempted to dissuade him from doing so as it was quite futile and he was only going to get an extra beating, Titus replied: 'Who knows? Perhaps something will stick.'

He prayed for them a lot, but he also seems to have considered it his duty to approach them in an attempt to bring them back to their sanity. More than once he encouraged his fellow prisoners by saying: 'We are here in a dark tunnel. We have to pass through it. Somewhere at the end shines the eternal light.'[96]

He spoke as much for the guards in their spiritual darkness as for the prisoners under their charge.

By the feast of Our Lady of Mount Carmel, on the 16th July, he was, one imagines, no longer working. He had been given a few days' respite after a brief visit to the 'hospital'. In the morning he had celebrated the Feast of the Carmelite Order and had received a Polish secular priest as a member of its Third Order. During the novena that preceded his initiation, Titus had given him a short talk. While walking outside he had placed his hand for a moment upon Tadeusz Zielinski's arm and told him that, if he were ever to be freed, he must renew his initiation solemnly. Titus must have felt happy that he could do this. Even in Dachau there were moments of respite. Even here, heaven and hell were curiously mingled.

The days of Titus's respite from work belong among the most cherished memories of Father Kuyper. The latter had met Titus in his parish at Rotterdam and remembered clearly the impact Titus had made on the people when he spoke about peace.[97] Father Kuyper had also been a chaplain in the forces and later became a dean in his diocese in Holland.

Father Kuyper was delighted to meet Professor Brandsma again, even in such tragic circumstances, and was touched to find Titus's spirit so untroubled. He was touched, too, by the optimism with which Titus still spoke of the work he hoped to finish at home. It was evident, in fact, to everyone who saw him now, that he could not go on much longer. He had already been pressed to go into the 'hospital' but, as some of them remembered, was not keen on the idea. Many were suspicious as to what went on there. And events have proved them right for Dr Rascher had set up an experimental station there where high pressure and exposure experiments were practised on defenceless prisoners. Another professor, Schilling, had his allotment of prisoners infected with malaria agents. Bio-chemical experiments were also carried out.

Father Kuyper was on the spot when Becker, the supervisor of Block 28, with his elbows leaning on the frame of an open window, bent down towards those inside. He seemed less maliciously humoured than usual and told Titus that he looked pretty ill. Later, before he was executed in 1945 for his war crimes, this man was to reconcile himself with God. Who knows at what moment the seeds of this reconciliation began to grow. It is not impossible that the prayers which Titus offered up for him began at some stage to have effect.

Now, at any rate, having looked him over carefully, Becker suggested that Titus had better go to the 'hospital'. Titus, for the first time without an argument, agreed. Father Kuyper was amazed at how readily he accepted the suggestion this time. Possibly Titus himself felt that he could not go on any longer. It is thought that he spent one or two more days in his barracks but this we cannot be sure of. All we know for certain is that one of those mornings he felt very ill. It was, as usual, early in the morning when, together with Tijhuis and a priest by the name of Rothkrans, Titus stood outside. It was cold and the rain was coming down in a steady drizzle. His companions looked round for a place to shelter. But this was not allowed. A guard rushed forward and, angry at their apparent indolence, beat them up. 'Then,' according to Father Rothkrans, 'Tijhuis, the Dutch Carmelite friar, went with Titus Brandsma to the prison hospital.'

With an encouraging word of thanks, Titus said good-bye to his colleague. There is no more evidence from the men in Block 28. It is at this point that the records leave off, for there was no means of contact with the 'hospital' and they never heard of, or saw, Titus again. The next thing they were to hear was the announcement of his death.

One has every reason to ask oneself what went on in Titus Brandsma's mind just before and just after he left for the 'hospital'.

One hears nothing about any words of farewell. What we do know is that he could barely stand on his feet any more, that he was exhausted and very ill, that he had been persuaded even by his own friends to go to the 'hospital', that it must have seemed to him the only place left to go to. And so, on that cold rainy morning, after having been beaten up, he was at the end of his tether and, supported by his colleague, he entered the camp 'hospital'.

He was to be there for only a matter of days, at the most a week. He lay there on a straw mattress on which so many had died before him. He had no room to himself, no crucifix at which to gaze. The care taken of him was minimal, but he was beyond human care.

A nurse, who must remain anonymous, has come forward of her own accord to bear witness to Titus Brandsma to whom she administered the deadly injection that was to put him out of his misery with the same casual effectiveness as if he were a suffering dog.

From her we know that he had been disgracefully humiliated by the doctors who experimented on him. It is neither fitting nor necessary to describe these experiments. While the doctors used his body for their own ends Titus merely said aloud: 'Not my will, but Thine be done.'

Titus had seriously talked to the assistant nurse and discovered that she came from Holland, and moreover from a Catholic home. 'How is it,' he had asked her, 'that you ended up here? I shall pray for you a great deal.'

He gave her his rosary at which she protested: 'But I can no longer pray.'

To this Titus retorted: 'Well, if you can't say the first part, surely you can still say Pray for us Sinners.'

She tried to excuse herself, and muttered something about 'so many bad priests'. Titus responded to her remark and asked her to observe the sufferings of the imprisoned priests around her. He even told her that he was glad to undergo his own sufferings for God's sake.

This nurse, whose name and address are known in Rome only, as her identity must remain secret on grounds of possible reprisals, has never forgotten her encounter with Titus Brandsma. She has returned to the practice of her Catholic religion.

A prominent Austrian, Dr Fritz Kühr, who survived the horrors of the camp, and was even given an administrative position at the 'hospital', had a couple of times taken Communion to Titus. He fell completely under the spell of his personality, even in these distressing circumstances. Kühr had to be extremely careful, of course, as he had no business to be with the patients.

The other patients were constantly seen to be surrounding Titus who tried to encourage and console them and direct their attention to God. But, for the last day or two, he was unconscious. Dr Kühr had twice slipped in to see if Titus could take Holy Communion, but he had found him beyond recall.

Dr Kühr gave his account to Father van Gestel, S.J., who was also a prisoner in the camp at Dachau and to whom we have already referred in connection with his article for the *Osservatore Romano* in which he gives the figures of the number of priests and ministers in Dachau in 1942. Through Dr Kühr he had exchanged a greeting with Titus while the latter was in the camp 'hospital'.

The nurse's final evidence concerns Titus's fatal injection. It was given on Sunday, the 26th July at 1.50 p.m. Ten minutes later, at 2 p.m., Titus Brandsma died.

His body was cremated three days later in the camp crematorium. It was with considerable emotion that the members of Block 28 learnt, that same Sunday afternoon, of Titus Brandsma's death. 'Heute nur Brandsma gestorben' ('Today only Brandsma died'), Becker had said.

Of those who were close to Brandsma the following lived to survive Dachau. They are: Raphael Tijhuis, O. Carm., P. van Gestel, S.J., Heinrich Rupieper, J. Rothkrans, Abbé Delcourt, L. De Coninck, and H. J. Kuyper.

They returned to their religious communities or dioceses after the liberation in 1945. The Protestant minister, Kapteyn, died in Dachau later that same year, in 1942.

There is nothing to be said for the sufferings of Dachau and camps like them, unless it is, perhaps, the compassion and understanding between men that they have generated in place of the hate that created them. There is little to remind us of the agony and desolation, and waste of human life and spirit that they represent except in stories like those of Titus Brandsma. But although we may, perhaps, be fortunate enough never to experience their like again they have not failed in human, as well as in spiritual, terms if they have served to show us how, in the most dire moments of sorrow, in the most agonizing moments of stress, there is always light at the end of the tunnel.

Notes

CHAPTER ONE

1. The name of Titus' grandmother was Apollonia Terwisscha van Scheltinga. (H. W. F. Aukes published a history in 1941 of the Catholic Frisian Generations: *Katholieke Friese geslachten* – Het Spectrum; Utrecht.)
2. Titus Brandsma, Us Fryske Aertbishop, *Utrechtse Courant*, 12.8.1933.
3. Doctors H. Oldenhof and M. J. Ydema, History of the parish Sensmeer-Blauwhuis, Bolsward (1951) 13th publication of *Frisia Catholica*.
4. *Ons Noorden*, October 1938, jubilee issue.
5. His sister Siebrig, whose religious name was Willibrorda, held the office of Assistant-General from 1919 to 1931 and was renowned for her holiness of life.

    Plone (Sister Barbara), the only surviving sister, resides at the Franciscan convent in Leeuwarden, the capital town of the province Friesland.

    The Bishop of Loeanfoe in China was Mgr Constans Kramer who presently lives in Holland.
6. Information by A. Hettema.
7. The results of these years are still available.
8. This chapter rests, apart from the sources already indicated, on information by Mrs G. de Boer-Brandsma; Henry Brandsma, O.F.M., and on information given by Titus himself. As for the period at Megen, information was furthermore given by former schoolmates.
9. According to Dr Booromaeus Tiecke, O. Carm.
10. Information from Henry Brandsma, O.F.M., and Aloysius van de Staay, O.Carm.
11. Based on *Courage to Build Anew*, edited by Edwina Fielding, ch. I; and on information from Carmelite Monastery, Ware, Herts.
12. Titus Brandsma, *The Beauty of Carmel*, lect. 1.

CHAPTER TWO

13. Prof. Dr Titus Brandsma, O.Carm., 'Klein Gedenkschrift' which was presented to Dr Hubertus Driessen, O.Carm. on the occasion of his golden jubilee as priest. Various colleagues had contributed to it by recalling their memories.

    Dr Hubertus Driessen was born 4th September, 1871 and died 29th October, 1946.

    Dr Hubertus had a brother who entered the same Order.

    He was Dr Eugenius Driessen who was born 8th March, 1876 and died 7th July, 1946. Dr Eugenius will be mentioned later in this chapter.

14. Titus Brandsma 'Klein Gedenkschrift'.
15. Dr Brocardus Meyer, O.Carm.
16. Titus Brandsma, contribution to 'Album Amicorum' presented to Dr Hubertus Driessen, 1937.
17. Dr Hubertus Driessen in 'Album Amicorum' presented to Titus Brandsma, 1939.
18. A. van de Staay, O.Carm.

CHAPTER THREE

19. Information A. van de Staay, O.Carm.; P. Lokkers, O.Carm., and others.
20. Titus Brandsma, *The Beauty of Carmel*, lect. 1.

CHAPTER FOUR

21. Telesphorus Kroonen who was to remain Provincial till 1909.

    Dr Hubertus Driessen was Provincial from 1909 to 1915; Dr Lambertus Smeets from 1915 to 1921, and Dr Cyprianus Verbeek from 1921 to 1930.

22. To his parents 20th November, 1906 and to the Provincial.
23. Collegio S. Alberto, Via Sforza Pallavicini, 10, Roma.
24. A. van de Staay.
25. To A. van de Staay, 18th December, 1900.
26. To family de Boer-Brandsma, 10th March, 1907.
27. To Dr H. Driessen, 19th May, 1909.

CHAPTER FIVE

28. To Dr H. Driessen, 14th August, 1909.
29. *Het Katholiek Sociaal Weekblad*.
30. The quotation is actually not from *Carmelrozen* but from *The Beauty of Carmel*, lect. 4.

31. *Werken der H. Teresia.* Her biography by T. Brandsma was published in 1918. *Her Foundations* by A. van Rijswijck was published in 1919. *The Road to Perfection* and *The Castle of the Soul* by T. Brandsma and A. van Rijswijck were published in 1926, while the first part of her letters by H. Driessen had been published in 1924.

32. 'In the Low Countries the ancient system of Canons of St Augustine came to new life in the congregation of Windesheim, to be the centre through all the fifteenth century of the new so-called *Devotio Moderna* and to be immortalized by a single book, which to this day is read by millions of all beliefs, the *Imitation of Christ*, the work of one of the canons, Thomas À Kempis. And with this same *Devotio Moderna* and Windesheim there is closely associated a wholly new order whose work lay in a new type of school for boys, the Brothers of the Common Life. From these schools came Nicholas of Cusa (1401–64), who, as an official reformer of Church life, is one of the really great men of the fifteenth century. Here the career of Erasmus had its first beginnings.' (*A Popular History Of The Reformation* by Philip Hughes.)

33. To J. van der Wey, 23rd October, 1919.

34. Titus Brandsma, *The Beauty of Carmel*, lect. 2.

35. Information from H. Brandsma, O.F.M., and correspondence with his mother.

36. To H. Driessen, 7th January, 1923 and already in the Spring of 1908 to A. van de Staay.

CHAPTER SIX

37. Opposition to the appointment of Dr Ferdinand Sassen came from one of the ministers in The Hague. A few years later Dr Sassen joined the professors' staff at Nijmegen.

38. According to the Year book of the Roman Catholic University 1923 to 1924, p. 74.

39. In the 'Spoorstraat'.

40. According to Dr B. Tiecke.

41. *A Dangerous Little Friar* by Josse Alzin.

42. 'In memoriam Titus Brandsma', in *De Volkskrant*, 30th July, 1960.

43. To Joseph Rees.

44. J. G. A. Mets, secretary of the St Boniface fraternity, as published in *Ons Noorden*, 4th September, 1930.

45. Information from Prof. Dr J. H. Brouwer, 10th August, 1942, who was present at the meeting between T. Brandsma and the Inspector, Mr Welling.

46. Statement by Prof. Dr K. L. Bellon, 16th October, 1956.

47. Prof. Dr Ferdinand Sassen in *De Gelderlander*, 2nd October, 1939.

48. *Some Memories of Titus Brandsma*, Dr B. Ter Ellen (Arch. Titus Brandsma).

CHAPTER SEVEN

49. Dr H. J. Denteneer, O.Carm. (Assistant to Titus Brandsma), 24th August, 1960.
50. Simon Besalduch, O.Carm., in a brief biography of Titus Brandsma in: *Flos Sancorum del Carmelo*, Barcelona 1951 (pp. 827–837).
51. 'Album Amicorum' to Dr H. Driessen, 1937.
52. To Joseph Rees.
53. Titus Brandsma, *The Beauty of Carmel* lect. 6.
54. Dr Brocardus Meyer.
55. To Joseph Rees.
56. Titus Brandsma, *The Beauty of Carmel*, lect. 3.
57. Titus Brandsma, *The Beauty of Carmel*, lect. 8.
58. The chairman, Mr H. F. A. Geise to Ir. Rosier, 24th February, 1944 (*Klein Gedenkschrift*, p. 151).
59. Mr H. F. A. Geise in 'De Gelderlander', 2nd October, 1939.
60. Address to the students of the St Olaf's Union at Tilburg, 28th October, 1936 and published in a special issue of the *Viking*.
61. Christopher Verhallen who was Titus' superior from 1936 to 1942, Dr M. Arts and others.
62. Amongst others: Dr M. Arts, O.Carm., Dr A. Nolte, O.Carm., Dr A. van de Staay, O.Carm., Dr B. Tiecke, O.Carm.
63. H. Van Keulen, C.S.S.R.
64. The Bishops Huibers of Haarlem and Jansen of Rotterdam.

CHAPTER EIGHT

65. To the family de Boer-Brandsma, 9th December, 1939 and 29th December, 1939.
66. Presently Cardinal Giobbe and Cardinal Agagianian.
67. College notes of Mrs dra. M. T. C. Elsberg-Kierwied.
68. Arch. Titus Brandsma.
69. Archbishop (later Cardinal) Jan De Jong came from the Isle of Ameland off the Frisian coast.

    H. W. F. Aukes published a biography of Cardinal de Jong in 1956 (*Kardinaal de Jong* – publ. 'Het Spectrum', Utrecht).

CHAPTER NINE

70. Information from Dr G. W. Gorris, S.J.

CHAPTER TEN

71. *Mijn Cell and Dagorde van een gevengene* – Titus Brandsma's cell memoirs, written between 23rd January and 31st January at Scheveningen and published with a brief introduction by Dr Brocardus Meyer, O.Carm.

72. *Mijn Cell* by Titus Brandsma.
73. Hardegen's whereabouts after the war have not been traced.
74. Titus Brandsma to J. J. Aalders.
75. 'Meldungen aus den Niederlanden' appeared in *Jahresbericht 1942*. A photocopy of the fragments concerned are in the Arch. Titus Brandsma.
76. *Mijn Cell* by Titus Brandsma.
77. 'Gott so nah und ferne. Gott ist immer da'.
78. L. Siegmund. (Arch. Titus Brandsma)
79. Titus's cell companion, C. de Graaf. (Arch. Titus Brandsma.)

CHAPTER ELEVEN

80. On 30th August, 1941 the Archbishop had written to Rauter to request admittance of priests in the concentration camp of Amersfoort. On 30th September, 1941 the SS Standartenführer und Oberst der Polizei, L. Harster replied that one had to expect that the Catholic clergy would receive rough treatment. Principal considerations, more-over, did not allow the request to be granted. (Arch. Archbishop.)
81. Dr C. P. Gunning in 'Op de Schoolbanken van de P.D.A.', 1946, p. 123.
82. Dr C. P. Gunning and the Protestant minister, Overduin, who sur-vived the war and produced much reliable evidence in his publications.
83. J. van de Mortel in a letter dated 1st February, 1955 (Arch. Titus Brandsma.)
84. J. J. A. Aalders.

CHAPTER TWELVE

85. Information, amongst others, from L. Siegmund and J. J. A. Aalders.
86. H. A. M. Nieuwenhoven in letters of 11th and 17th November, 1954. (Arch. Titus Brandsma) The two cell mates were: De Graaf and Oostdijk. The former has written his memoirs.
87. De Graaf.
88. Prior Chr. Verhallen. (Arch. Titus Brandsma)
89. Rijksinstituut van Oorlogsdocumentatie (photocopy in Arch. Titus Brandsma).

CHAPTER THIRTEEN

90. Report from the chaplain, L. Deimel. (Arch. Titus Brandsma)
91. Information from R. J. de Groot to Chr. Verhallen and also to Dr A. Staring. (Arch. Titus Brandsma)
92. Letter from Abbé Nic. Lamboras, Sourbrodt (Belgium), 14th August, 1955. (Arch. Titus Brandsma)

CHAPTER FOURTEEN

93. 'So was es in Dachau' by Mgr Joh. Neuhäusler (1960).
94. Rev. J. Janssen who was at the time a curate at Bleric.
95. Dr Jos. Kentenich, founder of the 'Schonstadtbewegung', later in Milwaukee USA, in a letter of 29th June, 1954. (Arch. Titus Brandsma)
96. Brother Raphael Tijhuis, O.Carm. and others.
97. Titus spoke many times in different places about peace and efforts for peace in the world. He was a member of the committee of the 'RK Vredesbond' (RC Union for Peace) which was founded on 7th November, 1925.

Appendix

A brief historical survey of the Carmelite Order:
There is no authentication for the tradition that the Carmelite Order originally began with non-Christian 'prophets' living on Mt Carmel. But it is generally accepted that by about A.D. 1150 a number of pilgrims and crusaders (both French and English) had settled on Mt Carmel to lead an eremitical life in imitation of the prophets. It was for their spiritual descendants that, in 1209, the Latin Patriarch of Jerusalem, St Albert, composed a rule (the Primitive Rule) which Pope Honorius III confirmed in 1226.

But sixty-five years later, in 1291, Acre and Mt Carmel were captured by the Seljuk Turks who massacred all the hermits they found there. Their absence lasted nearly four hundred years, for it was not until 1631 that any hermits returned to Mt Carmel. Many had already migrated to Europe in small groups before that fatal day in 1291. The first historical mention occurs in the early hermit foundation at Valenciennes (France) in 1235. They also made their way to England, and it was here particularly that the small foundations before 1247 badly lacked a secure juridical status and were regarded by other Mendicant Orders as intruders.

The hermits had brought their contemplative and prophetic character with them to England where they continued to live in hermitages. In consequence they could only live in the country and often found themselves insufficiently provided with necessities.

St Simon Stock, whose name is so much associated with the

Carmelite Order, but whose date of birth is unknown, was an Englishman. He had visited the Holy Land and returned to England with some hermits who are thought to have been former crusaders. At the General Chapter held at Aylesford in 1247 he was elected Sixth General of the entire Order. He asked for, and obtained from Rome, the necessary adaptations to the contemporary European conditions. Henceforth the monks could move into towns, share a monastic building, and take their meals in a common refectory.

St Simon Stock gave the Order a great impetus, although it was the next century that saw the Order really come into its own. It also achieved recognition as a Mendicant Order.

St Simon's vision of Our Lady bestowing the scapular has been mentioned in Chapter One (pages 11 and 12).

Due to the plague which afflicted Europe in the fourteenth and fifteenth centuries a relaxation from the Rule on certain points concerning penance, food, clothing, prayer, and silence was sought and, eventually, gained. For, in 1432, Pope Eugene IV approved a mitigated Rule. This later became known as the Calced Rule, in contrast to the Discalced Rule by St Teresa of Avila when she wished to return to the earlier, more austere Rule in the sixteenth century.

Both St Teresa and St John of the Cross in fact returned to the Primitive Rule of St Albert, though approving of the necessary adaptations and modifications made to it by St Simon Stock.

St Teresa had already launched her reform with the foundation of St Joseph's in Avila when, in 1567, she met St John of the Cross. As he, too, was in search of a more austere way of life she asked him to join her Discalced reform and help with the first foundation for men. To this he agreed.

In 1593 the Discalced were finally and officially separated from the Calced. The Discalced Rule is geared to a life of prayer and contemplation. For this reason it emphasizes silence and retirement. Perpetual abstinence from meat is observed and the Rule prescribes a fast of six months a year, from the feast of the Exaltation of the Holy Cross (14th September) until Easter. The literal meaning of the word 'discalced' is 'unshod', but in fact, for some time now, their members have worn sandals, although they originally went barefoot, an outward sign of the differences between them.

Titus Brandsma was, himself, a member of the Calced Carmelite Order.

Index

DATE DUE   (DA Pam 28-30)

DA FORM 1881, 1 JAN 57   ☆ GPO : 1960 OF-248-34